**ZONDERVAN**®

God's Words of Life for Men
Copyright © 1997 by Zondervan

Requests for information should be addressed to:
Zondervan. *Grand Rapids, Michigan 49530*

ISBN 978-0-310-81321-7

Excerpts taken from: *Men's Devotional Bible*, New International
Version. Copyright © 1993 by Zondervan

Project Manager: Kim Zeilstra
Design: The DesignWorks Group; cover, David Uttley;
        interior, Robin Black, www.thedesignworksgroup.com
Cover Image: Daryl Benson/Masterfile

Printed in China

08 09 10 11 12 13 14 15 • 12 11 10 9 8 7 6 5 4

GOD'S
WORDS *of* LIFE

FOR MEN

God's Words of Life on

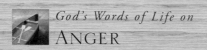

My dear brothers, take note of this: Everyone should be quick to listen, slow to speak and slow to become angry, for man's anger does not bring about the righteous life that God desires.

JAMES 1:19–20

Do not let the sun go down while you are still angry, and do not give the devil a foothold.

EPHESIANS 4:26–27

A gentle answer turns away wrath,
but a harsh word stirs up anger.

PROVERBS 15:1

A patient man has great understanding,
but a quick-tempered man displays folly.

PROVERBS 14:29

Better a patient man than a warrior,
a man who controls his temper than
one who takes a city.

PROVERBS 16:32

Do not take revenge, my friends, but leave room for God's wrath, for it is written: "It is mine to avenge; I will repay," says the Lord. On the contrary: "If your enemy is hungry, feed him; if he is thirsty, give him something to drink. In doing this, you will heap burning coals on his head." Do not be overcome by evil, but overcome evil with good.

ROMANS 12:19–21

Get rid of all bitterness, rage and anger, brawling and slander, along with every form of malice. Be kind and compassionate to one another, forgiving each other, just as in Christ God forgave you.

EPHESIANS 4:31–32

Jesus said, "I tell you that anyone who is angry with his brother will be subject to judgment. . . . Anyone who says, 'You fool!' will be in danger of the fire of hell."

MATTHEW 5:22

A wise man fears the LORD and shuns evil,
but a fool is hotheaded and reckless.
A quick-tempered man does foolish things,
and a crafty man is hated.

PROVERBS 14:16–17

God passed in front of Moses, proclaiming, "The LORD, the LORD, the compassionate and gracious God, slow to anger, abounding in love and faithfulness, maintaining love to thousands, and forgiving wickedness, rebellion and sin. Yet he does not leave the guilty unpunished; he punishes the children and their children for the sin of the fathers to the third and fourth generation."

EXODUS 34:6–7

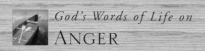

You must rid yourselves of all such things as these: anger, rage, malice, slander, and filthy language from your lips.

COLOSSIANS 3:8

A hot-tempered man stirs up dissension,
but a patient man calms a quarrel.

PROVERBS 15:18

Starting a quarrel is like breaching a dam;
so drop the matter before a dispute
breaks out.

PROVERBS 17:14

In your anger do not sin;
when you are on your beds,
search your hearts and be silent.

PSALM 4:4

Let the LORD judge the peoples.
Judge me, O LORD, according to
my righteousness,
according to my integrity,
O Most High.
My shield is God Most High,
who saves the upright in heart.

PSALM 7:8, 10

Sing to the LORD, you saints of his;
praise his holy name.
For his anger lasts only a moment,
but his favor lasts a lifetime;
weeping may remain for a night,
but rejoicing comes in the morning.

PSALM 30:4–5

*I will listen to what God the
LORD will say;
he promises peace to his
people, his saints—
but let them not return to folly.*

PSALM 85:8

*Though I walk in the midst of trouble,
you preserve my life;
you stretch out your hand against
the anger of my foes,
with your right hand you save me.
The LORD will fulfill his purpose for me;
your love, O LORD, endures forever—
do not abandon the works of your hands.*

PSALM 138:7–8

*Do not make friends with a hot-tempered man,
do not associate with one easily angered,
or you may learn his ways
and get yourself ensnared.*

PROVERBS 22:24–25

I want men everywhere to lift up holy hands in prayer, without anger or disputing.

1 TIMOTHY 2:8

Love is patient, love is kind. It does not envy, it does not boast, it is not proud. It is not rude, it is not self-seeking, it is not easily angered, it keeps no record of wrongs.

1 CORINTHIANS 13:4–5

Refrain from anger and turn from wrath;
> do not fret—it leads only to evil.

PSALM 37:8

If your enemy is hungry, give him food to eat;
> if he is thirsty, give him water to drink.
In doing this, you will heap
>   burning coals on his head,
> and the LORD will reward you.

PROVERBS 25:21–22

An angry man stirs up dissension,
> and a hot-tempered one commits many sins.
A man's pride brings him low,
> but a man of lowly spirit gains honor.

PROVERBS 29:22–23

Who is a God like you,
> who pardons sin and forgives the transgression
> of the remnant of his inheritance?
You do not stay angry forever
> but delight to show mercy.

MICAH 7:18

The LORD is compassionate and gracious,
> slow to anger, abounding in love.
He will not always accuse,
> nor will he harbor his anger forever.

PSALM 103:8–9

We live in an age of rage. By studying anger and its power, we can learn self-control so that we do not need to lose our temper in rage or abuse ourselves with resentment, but can defuse anger by resolving circumstances. We should reflect prayerfully about how we can incorporate these resolutions in our own lives:

To keep my life centered on God, as best I can, recognizing that when I do not, my natural self will generate things to become angry about.

To not condemn myself for feelings of anger.

To do everything I can to avoid acting on the basis of anger.

To clean up any problems I create as quickly as possible.

To redirect the energy of anger away from hurting people and toward improving conditions for people.

Each person who has sought God's help in the understanding and resolution of his or her anger has, without exception, received that help. There is, indeed, a miracle involved. It is the miracle of God's love for us, the miracle of his redemptive grace.

RICHARD P. WALTERS

Cast your cares on the LORD
and he will sustain you;
he will never let the righteous fall.

PSALM 55:22

Commit your way to the LORD;
trust in him and he will do this:
He will make your righteousness
shine like the dawn,
the justice of your cause
like the noonday sun.

PSALM 37:5–6

Commit to the LORD whatever you do,
and your plans will succeed.

PROVERBS 16:3

Jesus said, "Look at the birds of the air; they do not sow or reap or store away in barns, and yet your heavenly Father feeds them. Are you not much more valuable than they?"

MATTHEW 6:26

Do not be anxious about anything, but in everything, by prayer and petition, with thanksgiving, present your requests to God. And the peace of God, which transcends all understanding, will guard your hearts and your minds in Christ Jesus.

PHILIPPIANS 4:6–7

Blessed is the man who trusts in the LORD,
whose confidence is in him.
He will be like a tree planted by the water
that sends out its roots by the the stream.
It does not fear when heat comes;
its leaves are always green.
It has no worries in a year of drought
and never fails to bear fruit."

JEREMIAH 17:7–8

Keep your lives free from the love of money and be
content with what you have, because God has said,
"Never will I leave you; never will I forsake you."

HEBREWS 13:5

Jesus said, "Why do you worry about clothes?
See how the lilies of the field grow. They do not
labor or spin. Yet I tell you that not even Solomon
in all his splendor was dressed like one of these.
If that is how God clothes the grass of the field,
which is here today and tomorrow is thrown into
the fire, will he not much more clothe you, O you
of little faith?"

MATTHEW 6:28–30

Cast all your anxiety on him because he cares
for you.

1 PETER 5:7

Jesus said to his disciples: "Therefore I tell you, do
not worry about your life, what you will eat; or
about your body, what you will wear. Life is more
than food, and the body more than clothes."

LUKE 12:22–23

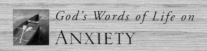
Jesus said, "Do not worry about tomorrow,
for tomorrow will worry about itself."

MATTHEW 6:34

Jesus said, "Seek first [God's] kingdom and his
righteousness, and all these things will be given to
you as well."

MATTHEW 6:33

The LORD himself goes before you and will be
with you; he will never leave you nor forsake you.
Do not be afraid; do not be discouraged.

DEUTERONOMY 31:8

The LORD said, "No one will be able to stand up
against you all the days of your life. As I was with
Moses, so I will be with you; I will never leave
you nor forsake you."

JOSHUA 1:5

Be strong and courageous. Do not be terrified;
do not be discouraged, for the LORD your God
will be with you wherever you go.

JOSHUA 1:9

Be on your guard; stand firm in the faith; be men
of courage; be strong.

1 CORINTHIANS 16:13

Let us then approach the throne of grace with
confidence, so that we may receive mercy and
find grace to help us in our time of need.

HEBREWS 4:16

We say with confidence, "The Lord is my helper;
I will not be afraid."

HEBREWS 13:6

God did not give us a spirit of timidity, but a spirit of power, of love and of self-discipline.

2 TIMOTHY 1:7

He who fears the LORD has a secure fortress,
and for his children it will be a refuge.

PROVERBS 14:26

The LORD is my shepherd, I shall not be in want.
He makes me lie down in green pastures,
he leads me beside quiet waters,
he restores my soul.
He guides me in paths of righteousness
for his name's sake.
Even though I walk
through the valley of the shadow of death,
I will fear no evil,
for you are with me;
your rod and your staff,
they comfort me.
You prepare a table before me
in the presence of my enemies.
You anoint my head with oil;
my cup overflows.
Surely goodness and love will follow me
all the days of my life,
and I will dwell in the house of the LORD
forever.

PSALM 23:1–6

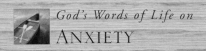
The LORD gives strength to his people;
　　the LORD blesses his people with peace.

PSALM 29:11

My flesh and my heart may fail,
　　but God is the strength of my heart
　　and my portion forever.

PSALM 73:26

Great peace have they who love your law,
　　and nothing can make them stumble.

PSALM 119:165

Those who trust in the LORD
　　　　are like Mount Zion,
　　which cannot be shaken but
　　　　endures forever.

PSALM 125:1

I pray that out of his glorious riches he may
strengthen you with power through his Spirit
in your inner being, so that Christ may dwell in
your hearts through faith. And I pray that you,
being rooted and established in love, may have
power, together with all the saints, to grasp how
wide and long and high and deep is the love of
Christ, and to know this love that surpasses
knowledge—that you may be filled to the
measure of all the fullness of God.

EPHESIANS 3:16–19

D o not be anxious," Paul writes to the Philippians. In one sense it is like telling a woman with a bad head cold not to sniffle and sneeze. Or maybe it is more like telling a wino to lay off the booze or a compulsive gambler to stay away from the track.

Is anxiety a disease or an addiction? Perhaps it is something of both. Partly, perhaps, because you can't help it, and partly because for some dark reason you choose not to help it, you torment yourself with detailed visions of the worst that can possibly happen.

Paul does not deny that the worst things will happen finally to all of us, as indeed he must have had a strong suspicion they were soon to happen to him. He does not try to minimize them. He does not try to explain them away as God's will or God's judgment or God's method of testing our spiritual fiber. He simply tells the Philippians that in spite of them—even in the thick of them—they are to keep in constant touch with the One who unimaginably transcends the worst things as he also unimaginably transcends the best.

FREDERICK BUECHNER

A man ought not to cover his head, since he is the image and glory of God; but the woman is the glory of man. For man did not come from woman, but woman from man; neither was man created for woman, but woman for man.

1 CORINTHIANS 11:7–9

Does not the very nature of things teach you that if a man has long hair, it is a disgrace to him, but that if a woman has long hair, it is her glory?

1 CORINTHIANS 11:14–15

When God created man, he made him in the likeness of God.

GENESIS 5:1

You made man ruler over the works of your hands;
you put everything under his feet:
all flocks and herds,
and the beasts of the field,
the birds of the air,
and the fish of the sea,
all that swim the paths of the seas.
O LORD, our LORD,
how majestic is your name
in all the earth!

PSALM 8:6–9

God said, "Let us make man in our image, in our likeness, and let them rule over the fish of the sea and the birds of the air, over the livestock, over all the earth, and over all the creatures that move along the ground." So God created man in his own image, in the image of God he created him; male and female he created them.

GENESIS 1:26–27

Yet, O LORD, you are our Father.
We are the clay, you are the potter;
we are all the work of your hand.

ISAIAH 64:8

If you have any encouragement from being united with Christ, if any comfort from his love, if any fellowship with the Spirit, if any tenderness and compassion, then make my joy complete by being like-minded, having the same love, being one in spirit and purpose. Do nothing out of selfish ambition or vain conceit, but in humility consider others better than yourselves. Each of you should look not only to your own interests, but also to the interests of others.

PHILIPPIANS 2:1–4

When the time had fully come, God sent his Son, born of a woman, born under law, to redeem those under law, that we might receive the full rights of sons. Because you are sons, God sent the Spirit of his Son into our hearts, the Spirit who calls out, "Abba, Father." So you are no longer a slave, but a son; and since you are a son, God has made you also an heir.

GALATIANS 4:4–7

There is a place where someone has testified:

What is man that you are mindful of him,
the son of man that you care for him?
You made him a little lower than the angels;
you crowned him with glory and honor
and put everything under his feet.

In putting everything under him, God left
nothing that is not subject to him. Yet at present
we do not see everything subject to him.

HEBREWS 2:6–8

He has showed you, O man, what is good.
And what does the Lord require of you?
To act justly and to love mercy
and to walk humbly with your God.

MICAH 6:8

Be on your guard; stand firm in the faith; be men
of courage; be strong. Do everything in love.

1 CORINTHIANS 16:13–14

When the angel of the LORD appeared to Gideon,
he said, "The LORD is with you, mighty warrior."

JUDGES 6:12

To a generation of men failed by their fathers and lost in a cloud of confusion, God says, "Don't spend a lifetime in aimless drifting. Don't succumb to mindless misinterpretations of masculine identity. Enter into a relationship with me, through Jesus Christ, and allow me to lead you into authentic manhood."

God wants us all to experience a deeper level of security. He wants emasculated men to become secure enough to confront timidity and fear, to take risks and make commitments. He wants macho men to become secure enough to crawl out from under the false pretensions and quit trying to impress people.

The freedom of authentic masculinity is an amazing thing to see. It produces a "divine elasticity" in men. Finally they can lead with firmness, then submit with humility. They can challenge with a cutting edge, then encourage with enthusiasm. They can fight aggressively for just causes, then moments later weep over suffering.

These are the masterpieces God had in mind when he created man. God looks at them and says, "Very good. You are magnificent creatures—and authentically male."

BILL HYBELS

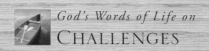
You will know that your children will be many,
and your descendants like the grass of the earth.
You will come to the grave in full vigor,
like sheaves gathered in season.

JOB 5:25–26

A man can do nothing better than to eat and drink and find satisfaction in his work. This too, I see, is from the hand of God, for without him, who can eat or find enjoyment? To the man who pleases him, God gives wisdom, knowledge and happiness, but to the sinner he gives the task of gathering and storing up wealth to hand it over to the one who pleases God. This too is meaningless, a chasing after the wind.

ECCLESIASTES 2:24–26

I thought, "Age should speak;
advanced years should teach wisdom."
But it is the spirit in a man,
the breath of the Almighty,
that gives him understanding.

JOB 32:7–8

The LORD said, "No one will be able to stand up against you all the days of your life. As I was with Moses, so I will be with you; I will never leave you nor forsake you."

JOSHUA 1:5

Even when I am old and gray,
do not forsake me, O God,
till I declare your power to the next generation,
your might to all who are to come.

PSALM 71:18

One thing I ask of the LORD,
    this is what I seek:
that I may dwell in the house of the LORD
    all the days of my life,
to gaze upon the beauty of the LORD
    and to seek him in his temple.

PSALM 27:4

They will still bear fruit in old age,
    they will stay fresh and green,
proclaiming, "The LORD is upright;
    he is my Rock, and there is no wickedness in him."

PSALM 92:14–15

Young men and maidens,
    old men and children.
Let them praise the name of the LORD,
    for his name alone is exalted;
    his splendor is above the
        earth and the heavens.

PSALM 148:12–13

Gray hair is a crown of splendor;
    it is attained by a righteous life.

PROVERBS 16:31

[God] has made everything beautiful in its time.
He has also set eternity in the hearts of men;
yet they cannot fathom what God has done from
beginning to end.

ECCLESIASTES 3:11

Remember your Creator
  in the days of your youth,
before the days of trouble come
  and the years approach when you will say,
  "I find no pleasure in them."

ECCLESIASTES 12:1

Even to your old age and gray hairs
  I am he, I am he who will sustain you.
I have made you and I will carry you;
  I will sustain you and I will rescue you.

ISAIAH 46:4

Man's days are determined;
  you have decreed the number of his months
  and have set limits he cannot exceed.

JOB 14:5

Honor your father and your mother, so that you
may live long in the land the LORD your God is
giving you.

EXODUS 20:12

He asked you for life, and you gave it to him—
  length of days, for ever and ever.

PSALM 21:4

Whoever of you loves life
  and desires to see many good days,
keep your tongue from evil
  and your lips from speaking lies.

PSALM 34:12–13

"With long life will I satisfy him
and show him my salvation," says the LORD.

PSALM 91:16

Keep my commands in your heart,
for they will prolong your life many years
and bring you prosperity.

PROVERBS 3:1–2

The fear of the LORD adds length to life,
but the years of the wicked are cut short.

PROVERBS 10:27

Whoever would love life
and see good days
must keep his tongue from evil
and his lips from deceitful speech.
He must turn from evil and do good;
he must seek peace and pursue it.

1 PETER 3:10–11

When I was a child, I talked like a child, I
thought like a child, I reasoned like a child.
When I became a man, I put childish ways
behind me.

1 CORINTHIANS 13:11

As for man, his days are like grass,
he flourishes like a flower of the field.

PSALM 103:15

Be strong in the Lord and in his mighty power.
Put on the full armor of God so that you can take
your stand against the devil's schemes. For our
struggle is not against flesh and blood, but against
the rulers, against the authorities, against the
powers of this dark world and against the
spiritual forces of evil in the heavenly realms.
Therefore put on the full armor of God, so that
when the day of evil comes, you may be able to
stand your ground, and after you have done
everything, to stand. Stand firm then, with the
belt of truth buckled around your waist, with the
breastplate of righteousness in place, and with
your feet fitted with the readiness that comes
from the gospel of peace. In addition to all this,
take up the shield of faith, with which you can
extinguish all the flaming arrows of the evil one.
Take the helmet of salvation and the sword of the
Spirit, which is the word of God.

EPHESIANS 6:10-17

I have examined America's breathless lifestyle and find it to be unacceptable. At forty-three years of age (I would be forty-four but I was sick a year), I have been thinking about the stages of my earthly existence and what they will represent at its conclusion. There was a time when all of my friends were graduating from high school. Now, it occurs to me that a time will soon come when my friends will be dying.

What does this have to do with my life today? How does it relate to yours? I'm suggesting that we stop and consider the brevity of our years on earth, perhaps finding new motivation to preserve the values that will endure. Why should we work ourselves into an early grave, missing those precious moments with loved ones who crave our affection and attention? It is a question that every man and woman should consider.

Let me offer this final word of encouragement for those who are determined to slow the pace: once you get out from under constant pressure, you'll wonder why you drove yourself so hard for all those years.

JAMES DOBSON

Jesus said, "In everything, do to others what you would have them do to you, for this sums up the Law and the Prophets."

MATTHEW 7:12

Jesus replied: "'Love the Lord your God with all your heart and with all your soul and with all your mind.' This is the first and greatest commandment. And the second is like it: 'Love your neighbor as yourself.' All the Law and the Prophets hang on these two commandments."

MATTHEW 22:37–40

The entire law is summed up in a single command: "Love your neighbor as yourself."

GALATIANS 5:14

LORD, who may dwell in your sanctuary?
    Who may live on your holy hill?
He whose walk is blameless
    and who does what is righteous,
who speaks the truth from his heart
    and has no slander on his tongue,
who does his neighbor no wrong
    and casts no slur on his fellowman,
who despises a vile man
    but honors those who fear the LORD,
who keeps his oath
    even when it hurts,
who lends his money without usury
    and does not accept a bribe
        against the innocent.
He who does these things
    will never be shaken.

PSALM 15:1–5

The fruit of the Spirit is love, joy, peace, patience, kindness, goodness, faithfulness, gentleness and self-control. Against such things there is no law.

GALATIANS 5:22–23

He has showed you, O man, what is good.
And what does the LORD require of you?
To act justly and to love mercy
and to walk humbly with your God.

MICAH 6:8

Who may ascend the hill of the LORD?
Who may stand in his holy place?
He who has clean hands and a pure heart,
who does not lift up his soul to an idol
or swear by what is false.

PSALM 24:3–4

Better a poor man whose walk is blameless
than a rich man whose ways are perverse.

PROVERBS 28:6

We also rejoice in our sufferings, because we know that suffering produces perseverance; perseverance, character; and character, hope.

ROMANS 5:3–4

Be careful that you do not forget the LORD your God, failing to observe his commands, his laws and his decrees.

DEUTERONOMY 8:11

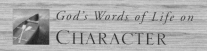
See to it that no one misses the grace of God and that no bitter root grows up to cause trouble and defile many.

HEBREWS 12:15

This is what the LORD says:
"Stand at the crossroads and look;
  ask for the ancient paths,
ask where the good way is, and walk in it,
  and you will find rest for your souls."

JEREMIAH 6:16

Evil men do not understand justice,
  but those who seek the LORD
    understand it fully.

PROVERBS 28:5

Blessed is the man
  who does not walk in the counsel of the wicked
or stand in the way of sinners
  or sit in the seat of mockers.
But his delight is in the law of the LORD,
  and on his law he meditates day and night.
He is like a tree planted by streams of water,
  which yields its fruit in season
and whose leaf does not wither.
  Whatever he does prospers.

PSALM 1:1–3

We continually remember before our God and Father your work produced by faith, your labor prompted by love, and your endurance inspired by hope in our Lord Jesus Christ.

1 THESSALONIANS 1:3

My dear friends, as you have always obeyed—not only in my presence, but now much more in my absence—continue to work out your salvation with fear and trembling, for it is God who works in you to will and to act according to his good purpose. Do everything without complaining or arguing so that you may become blameless and pure, children of God without fault in a crooked and depraved generation, in which you shine like stars in the universe.

PHILIPPIANS 2:12–15

My son, do not forget my teaching,
*   but keep my commands in your heart,*
for they will prolong your life many years
*   and bring you prosperity.*
Let love and faithfulness never leave you;
*   bind them around your neck,*
*   write them on the tablet of your heart.*
Then you will win favor and a good name
*   in the sight of God and man.*
Trust in the LORD with all your heart
*   and lean not on your own understanding;*
in all your ways acknowledge him,
*   and he will make your paths straight.*
Do not be wise in your own eyes;
*   fear the LORD and shun evil.*
This will bring health to your body
*   and nourishment to your bones.*

PROVERBS 3:1–8

Jesus said, "Do to others as you would have them do to you."

LUKE 6:31

Young men, . . . be submissive to those who are
older. All of you, clothe yourselves with humility
toward one another, because, "God opposes the
proud but gives grace to the humble."

1 PETER 5:5

The noble man makes noble plans,
and by noble deeds he stands.

ISAIAH 32:8

The wisdom of the prudent is
to give thought to their ways,
but the folly of fools is deception.
Fools mock at making amends for sin,
but goodwill is found among the upright.

PROVERBS 14:8–9

To the man who pleases him, God gives wisdom,
knowledge and happiness, but to the sinner he
gives the task of gathering and storing up wealth
to hand it over to the one who pleases God. This
too is meaningless, a chasing after the wind.

ECCLESIASTES 2:26

Dear friends, I urge you, as aliens and strangers in
the world, to abstain from sinful desires, which
war against your soul. Live such good lives among
the pagans that, though they accuse you of doing
wrong, they may see your good deeds and glorify
God on the day he visits us.

1 PETER 2:11

Let us consider how we may spur one another on toward love and good deeds. Let us not give up meeting together, as some are in the habit of doing, but let us encourage one another—and all the more as you see the Day approaching.

HEBREWS 10:24

Consider it pure joy, my brothers, whenever you face trials of many kinds, because you know that the testing of your faith develops perseverance. Perseverance must finish its work so that you may be mature and complete, not lacking anything. If any of you lacks wisdom, he should ask God, who gives generously to all without finding fault, and it will be given to him. But when he asks, he must believe and not doubt, because he who doubts is like a wave of the sea, blown and tossed by the wind. That man should not think he will receive anything from the Lord; he is a double-minded man, unstable in all he does. Blessed is the man who perseveres under trial, because when he has stood the test, he will receive the crown of life that God has promised to those who love him.

JAMES 1:2–8, 12

Do not merely listen to the word, and so deceive yourselves. Do what it says. Anyone who listens to the word but does not do what it says is like a man who looks at his face in a mirror and, after looking at himself, goes away and immediately forgets what he looks like. But the man who looks intently into the perfect law that gives freedom, and continues to do this, not forgetting what he has heard, but doing it—he will be blessed in what he does.

JAMES 1:22-25

Love the LORD your God with all your heart and with all your soul and with all your strength. These commandments that I give you today are to be upon your hearts.

DEUTERONOMY 6:5-6

Aristotle defined character as the decisions a person makes when the choice is not obvious. My father used to say, "Character is the way we act when nobody's looking."

For example, it's no test of character to stop your car at a police roadblock. The test comes, rather, when you're driving at 4 A.M. along a desolate back road in Iowa. You're heading toward a red light at a deserted intersection and you can see for miles around that there's nobody else on the roads. Do you obey the law? This is a test of character, a choice made on the basis of respect for law, on the discipline of adhering to the principles of safe driving. You decide to stop on the strength of character instead of responding to convenience or whim.

Of course, to the person who is well disciplined in respect for law, as well as other ethical and moral principles, such a simple illustration of choice is automatically invalid. For such a person, the only course of action is already established because you stop at red lights; that's all there is to it, whatever the time or traffic conditions. You do what is right, not what you know to be wrong.

D. BRUCE LOCKERBIE

Jesus said, "You have heard that it was said to the people long ago, 'Do not break your oath, but keep the oaths you have made to the Lord.' But I tell you, Do not swear at all: either by heaven, for it is God's throne; or by the earth, for it is his footstool; or by Jerusalem, for it is the city of the Great King. And do not swear by your head, for you cannot make even one hair white or black. Simply let your 'Yes' be 'Yes,' and your 'No,' 'No'; anything beyond this comes from the evil one.

MATTHEW 5:33–37

Do not conform any longer to the pattern of this world, but be transformed by the renewing of your mind. Then you will be able to test and approve what God's will is—his good, pleasing and perfect will.

ROMANS 12:2

Jesus said, "Whoever acknowledges me before men, I will also acknowledge him before my Father in heaven. But whoever disowns me before men, I will disown him before my Father in heaven."

MATTHEW 10:32–33

See, I am setting before you today a blessing and a curse—the blessing if you obey the commands of the LORD your God that I am giving you today; the curse if you disobey the commands of the LORD your God and turn from the way that I command you today by following other gods.

DEUTERONOMY 11:26–28

Samuel replied:

"Does the LORD delight in burnt
offerings and sacrifices
as much as in obeying the voice of the Lord?
To obey is better than sacrifice,
and to heed is better than the fat of rams."

1 SAMUEL 15:22

Jesus said, "I am the true vine, and my Father is
the gardener. He cuts off every branch in me that
bears no fruit, while every branch that does bear
fruit he prunes so that it will be even more
fruitful. You are already clean because of the word
I have spoken to you. Remain in me, and I will
remain in you. No branch can bear fruit by itself;
it must remain in the vine. Neither can you bear
fruit unless you remain in me. I am the vine; you
are the branches. If a man remains in me and I in
him, he will bear much fruit; apart from me you
can do nothing. If anyone does not remain in me,
he is like a branch that is thrown away and
withers; such branches are picked up, thrown into
the fire and burned. If you remain in me and my
words remain in you, ask whatever you wish, and
it will be given you."

JOHN 15:1–7

I will give them singleness of heart and action, so that they will always fear me for their own good and the good of their children after them. I will make an everlasting covenant with them: I will never stop doing good to them, and I will inspire them to fear me, so that they will never turn away from me.

JEREMIAH 32:39–40

I am convinced that neither death nor life, neither angels nor demons, neither the present nor the future, nor any powers, neither height nor depth, nor anything else in all creation, will be able to separate us from the love of God that is in Christ Jesus our Lord.

ROMANS 8:38–39

When the kindness and love of God our Savior appeared, he saved us, not because of righteous things we had done, but because of his mercy. He saved us through the washing of rebirth and renewal by the Holy Spirit, whom he poured out on us generously through Jesus Christ our Savior, so that, having been justified by his grace, we might become heirs having the hope of eternal life. This is a trustworthy saying. And I want you to stress these things, so that those who have trusted in God may be careful to devote themselves to doing what is good. These things are excellent and profitable for everyone.

TITUS 3:4–8

A well-known national television talk-show host once invited a minister of the gospel on his program. At one point the talk-show host asked the man of God why Christians were so narrow-minded in thinking that they were the only people in the whole world who knew God and who knew they were going to heaven.

The minister quoted scripture: "I am the way and the truth and the life. No one comes to the Father except through me" (John 14:6).

The preacher then stated, "I didn't say that, God did. If you don't agree with it, tell him, not me."

That's also the answer for training camp Christians [those who attempt to barter with God to achieve success]. The promises made, but not kept; the functions attended, but not experienced; the hopes dreamed, but not put into action—commitment matters. There is no success for a football player—or a Christian—without it.

Reggie White

The LORD is my light and my salvation—
whom shall I fear?
The LORD is the stronghold of my life—
of whom shall I be afraid?

PSALM 27:1

So do not fear, for I am with you;
do not be dismayed, for I am your God.
I will strengthen you and help you;
I will uphold you with my righteous right hand.

ISAIAH 41:10

I can do everything through Christ who gives
me strength.

PHILIPPIANS 4:13

Dear friends, do not be surprised at the painful
trial you are suffering, as though something
strange were happening to you. But rejoice that
you participate in the sufferings of Christ, so that
you may be overjoyed when his glory is revealed.

1 PETER 4:12–13

When you pass through the waters,
I will be with you;
and when you pass through the rivers,
they will not sweep over you.
When you walk through the fire,
you will not be burned;
the flames will not set you ablaze.
For I am the LORD, your God,
the Holy One of Israel, your Savior; . . .
Since you are precious and honored in my sight.

ISAIAH 43:2–4

In all these things we are more than conquerors
through him who loved us. For I am convinced
that neither death nor life, neither angels nor
demons, neither the present nor the future, nor
any powers, neither height nor depth, nor
anything else in all creation, will be able to
separate us from the love of God that is in Christ
Jesus our Lord.

ROMANS 8:37–39

Wait for the LORD;
be strong and take heart
and wait for the LORD.

PSALM 27:14

How great is your goodness,
which you have stored up for those who fear you,
which you bestow in the sight of men
on those who take refuge in you.
In the shelter of your presence you hide them
from the intrigues of men;
in your dwelling you keep them safe
from accusing tongues.
Be strong and take heart,
all you who hope in the LORD.

PSALM 31:19-20, 24

Have I not commanded you? Be strong and
courageous. Do not be terrified; do not be
discouraged, for the LORD your God will be with
you wherever you go.

JOSHUA 1:9

God gives strength to the weary
and increases the power of the weak.
Even youths grow tired and weary,
and young men stumble and fall;
but those who hope in the LORD
will renew their strength.
They will soar on wings like eagles;
they will run and not grow weary,
they will walk and not be faint.

ISAIAH 40:29–31

Do not be anxious about anything, but in everything, by prayer and petition, with thanksgiving, present your requests to God. And the peace of God, which transcends all understanding, will guard your hearts and your minds in Christ Jesus.

PHILIPPIANS 4:6–7

Strengthen the feeble hands,
steady the knees that give way;
say to those with fearful hearts,
"Be strong, do not fear;
your God will come,
he will come with vengeance."

ISAIAH 35:3–4

Jesus said, "I have prayed for you, that your faith may not fail. And when you have turned back, strengthen your brothers."

LUKE 22:32

"I am about to go the way of all the earth,"
David said. "So be strong, show yourself a man,
and observe what the LORD your God requires:
Walk in his ways, and keep his decrees and
commands, his laws and requirements, as written
in the Law of Moses, so that you may prosper in
all you do and wherever you go."

1 KINGS 2:2–3

You will have success if you are careful to observe
the decrees and laws that the LORD gave Moses
for Israel. Be strong and courageous. Do not be
afraid or discouraged.

1 CHRONICLES 22:13

Be strong in the Lord and in his mighty power.

EPHESIANS 6:10

Our fathers disciplined us for a little while as they
thought best; but God disciplines us for our good,
that we may share in his holiness. No discipline
seems pleasant at the time, but painful. Later on,
however, it produces a harvest of righteousness
and peace for those who have been trained by it.
Therefore, strengthen your feeble arms and weak
knees. "Make level paths for your feet," so that the
lame may not be disabled, but rather healed.

HEBREWS 12:10–13

Be strong and very courageous. Be careful to obey
all the law my servant Moses gave you; do not
turn from it to the right or to the left, that you
may be successful wherever you go.

JOSHUA 1:7

Be on your guard; stand firm in the faith; be men of courage; be strong.

1 CORINTHIANS 16:13

Be strong and courageous. Do not be afraid or terrified because of them, for the LORD your God goes with you; he will never leave you nor forsake you.

DEUTERONOMY 31:6

Act with courage, and may the LORD be with those who do well.

2 CHRONICLES 19:11

Jesus immediately said to them: "Take courage! It is I. Don't be afraid."

MATTHEW 14:27

To live is Christ and to die is gain.

PHILIPPIANS 1:21

I love you, O LORD, my strength.
The LORD is my rock, my
         fortress and my deliverer;
    my God is my rock,
         in whom I take refuge.
He is my shield and the horn of
    my salvation, my stronghold.

PSALM 18:1–2

I t takes courage to look your spouse in the eye and say, "Our marriage is in serious trouble, and we've got to do something about it."

What do most people do? They put their problems on the back burner and go their own directions. While they pursue their own careers and their own recreations, the marriage disintegrates from lack of courage. They did not have the courage to put on the gloves and say, "Let's fight for this marriage." It takes courage to fight off the "greener grass" temptations, to work through layer after layer of masks, cover-ups, and defense mechanisms. Relational courage does not apply only to the husband-wife relationship. . . .

It also takes relational courage to build significant relationships with friends, to look another person in the eye and say, "Isn't it time we stopped talking about the weather and the stock market and started talking about what's going on in your life and mine?"

Not many men have the courage to challenge each other, to fight for each other's spiritual and relational growth. But I have learned over the years that I will never be a success in my marriage, with my kids or with my friends, without courage. BILL HYBELS

You heard my cry for mercy
      when I called to you for help.
Be strong and take heart,
      all you who hope in the LORD.

PSALM 31:22, 24

Cast your cares on the LORD
      and he will sustain you;
      he will never let the righteous fall.

PSALM 55:22

Do not be anxious about anything, but in
everything, by prayer and petition, with
thanksgiving, present your requests to God.
And the peace of God, which transcends all
understanding, will guard your hearts and your
minds in Christ Jesus.

PHILIPPIANS 4:6–7

In my distress I called to the LORD,
      and he answered me.
From the depths of the grave I called for help,
      and you listened to my cry.

JONAH 2:2

My tears have been my food
      day and night,
while men say to me all day long,
      "Where is your God?"
Why are you downcast, O my soul?
      Why so disturbed within me?
Put your hope in God,
      for I will yet praise him,
      my Savior and my God.

PSALM 42:3, 5–6

Answer me quickly, O LORD;
my spirit fails.
Do not hide your face from me
or I will be like those who go down to the pit.
Let the morning bring me word
of your unfailing love,
for I have put my trust in you.
Show me the way I should go,
for to you I lift up my soul.

PSALM 143:7–8

The LORD is a refuge for the oppressed,
a stronghold in times of trouble.

PSALM 9:9

The eternal God is your refuge,
and underneath are the everlasting arms.

DEUTERONOMY 33:27

You are my lamp, O LORD;
the LORD turns my darkness into light.

2 SAMUEL 22:29

A righteous man may have many troubles,
but the LORD delivers him from them all.

PSALM 34:19

Jesus said, "Look at the birds of the air; they do
not sow or reap or store away in barns, and yet
your heavenly Father feeds them. Are you not
much more valuable than they?"

MATTHEW 6:26

If the LORD delights in a man's way,
>   he makes his steps firm;
though he stumble, he will not fall,
>   for the LORD upholds him with his hand.
>   PSALM 37:23–24

God is our refuge and strength,
>   an ever-present help in trouble.
Therefore we will not fear, though the earth give way
>   and the mountains fall into the heart of the sea,
though its waters roar and foam
>   and the mountains quake with their surging.
>   PSALM 46:1–3

Though you have made me see
>   troubles, many and bitter,
>   you will restore my life again;
from the depths of the earth
>   you will again bring me up.
>   PSALM 71:20

My flesh and my heart may fail,
>   but God is the strength of my heart
>   and my portion forever.
>   PSALM 73:26

Even youths grow tired and weary,
>   and young men stumble and fall;
but those who hope in the LORD
>   will renew their strength.
They will soar on wings like eagles;
>   they will run and not grow weary,
>   they will walk and not be faint.
>   ISAIAH 40:30–31

So do not fear, for I am with you;
  do not be dismayed, for I am your God.
I will strengthen you and help you;
  I will uphold you with my
    righteous right hand.

ISAIAH 41:10

When you pass through the waters,
  I will be with you;
and when you pass through the rivers,
  they will not sweep over you.
When you walk through the fire,
  you will not be burned;
  the flames will not set you ablaze.

ISAIAH 43:2

Jesus said, "Do not let your hearts be troubled.
Trust in God; trust also in me."

JOHN 14:1

"I will refresh the weary and satisfy the faint,"
says the LORD.

JEREMIAH 31:25

We are hard pressed on every side, but not
crushed; perplexed, but not in despair; persecuted,
but not abandoned; struck down, but not
destroyed. Therefore we do not lose heart.
Though outwardly we are wasting away, yet
inwardly we are being renewed day by day.

2 CORINTHIANS 4:8–9, 16

Jesus said, "I have told you these things, so that in
me you may have peace. In this world you will have
trouble. But take heart! I have overcome the world."

JOHN 16:33

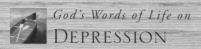

As for God, his way is perfect;
    the word of the Lord is flawless.
He is a shield
    for all who take refuge in him.
For who is God besides the LORD?
    And who is the Rock except our God?
It is God who arms me with strength
    and makes my way perfect.
He makes my feet like the feet of a deer;
    he enables me to stand on the heights.
                    PSALM 18:30–33

Whenever anyone turns to the Lord, the veil is
taken away. Now the Lord is the Spirit, and
where the Spirit of the Lord is, there is freedom.
          2 CORINTHIANS 3:16–17

If you will look to God
    and plead with the Almighty,
if you are pure and upright,
    even now he will rouse himself on your behalf
    and restore you to your rightful place.
                    JOB 8:5–6

Create in me a pure heart, O God,
    and renew a steadfast spirit within me.
Do not cast me from your presence
    or take your Holy Spirit from me.
Restore to me the joy of your salvation
    and grant me a willing spirit, to sustain me.
                 PSALM 51:10–12

L ife is composed of experiences which provide both challenge to one's character and the testing of one's spirit.

In 1 Kings 19, I see a defeated and desolate Elijah sitting under a broom tree in the solitude of his own sadness. He had to ask life's most difficult question: "How did I get to where I am, which is so far from where I am supposed to be?"

There are only three kinds of people in the world: those who are in the wilderness, those who have just come out of the wilderness, and those who are headed into the wilderness. In the midst of Elijah's wilderness experience, God sent his angel to feed him. "You don't have enough for your journey."

"What journey? I'm through. I'm all washed up."

"You're not through yet, Elijah. I'm going to send you from where you are to where I want you to be. I'm going to send you from the wilderness to the mountain."

In the wilderness there is weakness, but on the mountain there is strength. In the wilderness there is despair, but on the mountain there is hope.

H. BEECHER HICKS

I urge you, brothers, in view of God's mercy, to offer your bodies as living sacrifices, holy and pleasing to God—this is your spiritual act of worship. Do not conform any longer to the pattern of this world, but be transformed by the renewing of your mind. Then you will be able to test and approve what God's will is—his good, pleasing and perfect will.

ROMANS 12:1–2

Jesus said, "Anyone who loves his father or mother more than me is not worthy of me; anyone who loves his son or daughter more than me is not worthy of me; and anyone who does not take his cross and follow me is not worthy of me. Whoever finds his life will lose it, and whoever loses his life for my sake will find it."

MATTHEW 10:37–39

LORD, *who may dwell in your sanctuary?*
Who may live on your holy hill?
He whose walk is blameless
and who does what is righteous,
who speaks the truth from his heart.

PSALM 15:1–2

He who walks righteously
and speaks what is right,
who rejects gain from extortion
and keeps his hand from accepting bribes,
who stops his ears against plots of murder
and shuts his eyes against contemplating evil—
this is the man who will dwell on the heights.

ISAIAH 33:15–16

The fruit of righteousness will be peace;
  the effect of righteousness
    will be quietness and
    confidence forever.
                      ISAIAH 32:17

Is not this the kind of fasting I have chosen:
to loose the chains of injustice
  and untie the cords of the yoke,
to set the oppressed free and break every yoke?
Is it not to share your food with the hungry
  and to provide the poor
      wanderer with shelter—
when you see the naked, to clothe him,
  and not to turn away from
      your own flesh and blood?
Then your light will break forth like the dawn,
  and your healing will quickly appear;
then your righteousness will go before you,
  and the glory of the LORD
      will be your rear guard.
                      ISAIAH 58:6–8

Jesus said, "Remain in me, and I will remain in
you. No branch can bear fruit by itself; it must
remain in the vine. Neither can you bear fruit
unless you remain in me. I am the vine; you are
the branches. If a man remains in me and I in
him, he will bear much fruit; apart from me you
can do nothing."
                      JOHN 15:4–5

Those who live in accordance with the Spirit have
their minds set on what the Spirit desires.
                      ROMANS 8:5

He follows my decrees
and faithfully keeps my laws.
That man is righteous;
he will surely live,
declares the Sovereign LORD.

EZEKIEL 18:9

He has showed you, O man, what is good.
And what does the LORD require of you?
To act justly and to love mercy
and to walk humbly with your God.

MICAH 6:8

Jesus said, "Whoever lives by the truth comes
into the light, so that it may be seen plainly that
what he has done has been done through God."

JOHN 3:21

Jesus said, "By this all men will know that you are
my disciples, if you love one another."

JOHN 13:35

Jesus replied, "If anyone loves me, he will obey
my teaching. My Father will love him, and we
will come to him and make our home with him."

JOHN 14:23

The one who sows to please the Spirit, from the
Spirit will reap eternal life. Let us not become
weary in doing good, for at the proper time we
will reap a harvest if we do not give up.

GALATIANS 6:8–9

One thing I do: Forgetting what is behind and
straining toward what is ahead, I press on toward
the goal to win the prize for which God has
called me heavenward in Christ Jesus.

PHILIPPIANS 3:13–14

The grace of God that brings salvation has appeared
to all men. It teaches us to say "No" to ungodliness
and worldly passions, and to live self-controlled,
upright and godly lives in this present age.

TITUS 2:11–12

Religion that God our Father accepts as pure and
faultless is this: to look after orphans and widows
in their distress and to keep oneself from being
polluted by the world.

JAMES 1:27

Jesus said, "Everyone who hears these words of
mine and puts them into practice is like a wise
man who built his house on the rock. The rain
came down, the streams rose, and the winds blew
and beat against that house; yet it did not fall,
because it had its foundation on the rock."

MATTHEW 7:24–25

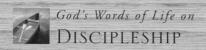
Jesus said, "Blessed are those who are persecuted because of righteousness, for theirs is the kingdom of heaven. Blessed are you when people insult you, persecute you and falsely say all kinds of evil against you because of me. Rejoice and be glad, because great is your reward in heaven, for in the same way they persecuted the prophets who were before you. You are the salt of the earth. . . . You are the light of the world. . . . Let your light shine before men, that they may see your good deeds and praise your Father in heaven."

MATTHEW 5:10–14, 16

All my life I had made my football career the number-one priority and let it dictate the direction of my life. Now here in Matthew 7:24–25 the Bible was saying I needed to make God and his will first and follow his direction for my life.

The crossroads I faced in my life was really a spiritual crossroads. I had to decide whether or not I believed what the Bible said. All my other questions hung on that one decision. But I finally reached a point where faith outweighed the doubts, and I was willing to commit my entire life to God.

I can't say that decision made an immediately visible difference in my life. I can't even say it instantly transformed me into a much better person; I had a lot yet to learn—and I still do—about how God wants me to live my life.

But what my new Christian experience did for me was to place football behind the priorities of my faith and my family and give me a sense of confidence and peace about the future—whatever it would be.

TOM LANDRY

I denied myself nothing my eyes desired;
> *I refused my heart no pleasure.*
My heart took delight in all my work,
> *and this was the reward for all my labor.*
Yet when I surveyed all that
> > *my hands had done*
> *and what I had toiled to achieve,*
everything was meaningless, a chasing after the wind;
> *nothing was gained under the sun.*

ECCLESIASTES 2:10–11

Be on your guard; stand firm in the faith; be men of courage; be strong. Do everything in love.

1 CORINTHIANS 16:13–14

This is what the LORD Almighty says: "Give careful thought to your ways."

HAGGAI 1:5

I urge you, brothers, in view of God's mercy, to offer your bodies as living sacrifices, holy and pleasing to God—this is your spiritual act of worship. Do not conform any longer to the pattern of this world, but be transformed by the renewing of your mind. Then you will be able to test and approve what God's will is—his good, pleasing and perfect will.

ROMANS 12:1–2

Jesus said, "If you love those who love you, what credit is that to you? Even 'sinners' love those who love them. And if you do good to those who are good to you, what credit is that to you? Even 'sinners' do that. And if you lend to those from whom you expect repayment, what credit is that to you? Even 'sinners' lend to 'sinners,' expecting to be repaid in full. But love your enemies, do good to them, and lend to them without expecting to get anything back. Then your reward will be great, and you will be sons of the Most High."

LUKE 6:32–35

We who are strong ought to bear with the failings of the weak and not to please ourselves. Each of us should please his neighbor for his good, to build him up.

ROMANS 15:1–2

Carry each other's burdens, and in this way you will fulfill the law of Christ. If anyone thinks he is something when he is nothing, he deceives himself.

GALATIANS 6:2–3

Each of you should look not only to your own interests, but also to the interests of others. Your attitude should be the same as that of Christ Jesus.

PHILIPPIANS 2:4–5

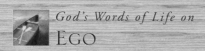
If anyone has material possessions and sees his brother in need but has no pity on him, how can the love of God be in him? Dear children, let us not love with words or tongue but with actions and in truth.

1 JOHN 3:17–18

Nobody should seek his own good, but the good of others.

1 CORINTHIANS 10:24

Love is patient, love is kind. It does not envy, it does not boast, it is not proud. It is not rude, it is not self-seeking, it is not easily angered, it keeps no record of wrongs.

1 CORINTHIANS 13:4–5

Even youths grow tired and weary,
*   and young men stumble and fall;*
but those who hope in the LORD
*   will renew their strength.*
They will soar on wings like eagles;
*   they will run and not grow weary,*
*   they will walk and not be faint.*

ISAIAH 40:30–31

If you really keep the royal law found in Scripture, "Love your neighbor as yourself," you are doing right.

JAMES 2:8

You meet so many small men! Not small in stature—but men who think little, talk little, plan little. Like eagles staked to the ground, there's no soar to them. Ceiling is zero—and their horizons are pulled in to the hub.

Not that these men are selfish (some of course are). But it's just that they're preoccupied most of the time with their own little bailiwick. They don't allow their minds to stretch and breathe. They don't think—they just rearrange their prejudices.

These little men are indifferent to problems other than their own. They have no concern for those things which do not hold a personal reference. They refuse to be bothered!

The times demand big men. Not men who are big shots (they're useless), but men who are big in heart and mind. Great men! Large-souled men!

Men with a vision—whose feet are on the ground but whose eyes are on the far horizon. Men whose hearts God has touched. Men committed—dedicated to God and his holy, high purposes! Men of integrity!

RICHARD HALVERSON

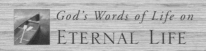
God has given us eternal life, and this life is in his Son.

1 JOHN 5:11

Jesus said, "I tell you the truth, whoever hears my word and believes him who sent me has eternal life and will not be condemned; he has crossed over from death to life."

JOHN 5:24

Jesus said, "God so loved the world that he gave his one and only Son, that whoever believes in him shall not perish but have eternal life."

JOHN 3:16

Jesus answered, "I tell you the truth, he who believes has everlasting life."

JOHN 6:47

Jesus said, "Whoever drinks the water I give him will never thirst. Indeed, the water I give him will become in him a spring of water welling up to eternal life."

JOHN 4:14

We know also that the Son of God has come and has given us understanding, so that we may know him who is true. And we are in him who is true—even in his Son Jesus Christ. He is the true God and eternal life.

1 JOHN 5:20

Surely goodness and love will follow me
all the days of my life,
and I will dwell in the house of the LORD
forever.

PSALM 23:6

My brothers, I want you to know that through
Jesus the forgiveness of sins is proclaimed to you.
Through him everyone who believes is justified
from everything you could not be justified from
by the law of Moses.

ACTS 13:38–39

Jesus said to her, "I am the resurrection and the
life. He who believes in me will live, even though
he dies; and whoever lives and believes in me will
never die."

JOHN 11:25–26

Jesus answered, "My sheep listen to my voice;
I know them, and they follow me. I give them
eternal life, and they shall never perish; no one
can snatch them out of my hand."

JOHN 10:27–28

Praise be to the God and Father of our Lord Jesus
Christ! In his great mercy he has given us new
birth into a living hope through the resurrection
of Jesus Christ from the dead.

1 PETER 1:3

If you confess with your mouth, "Jesus is Lord,"
and believe in your heart that God raised him
from the dead, you will be saved. For it is with
your heart that you believe and are justified, and
it is with your mouth that you confess and are
saved. As the Scripture says, "Anyone who trusts
in him will never be put to shame." For there is
no difference between Jew and Gentile—the same
Lord is Lord of all and richly blesses all who call
on him, for, "Everyone who calls on the name of
the Lord will be saved."

ROMANS 10:9–13

Then know this, you and all the people of Israel:
It is by the name of Jesus Christ of Nazareth,
whom you crucified but whom God raised from
the dead, that this man stands before you healed.
He is "the stone you builders rejected, which has
become the capstone." Salvation is found in no
one else, for there is no other name under heaven
given to men by which we must be saved.

ACTS 4:10–12

Father of glory,
How I thank you for the assurance of
heaven! While I know I could never deserve
such an assurance, I'm so grateful that you even
give it to me as a right because of my union
with your Son, my Savior.

Thank you that while I live in the world I
can seek to serve you fruitfully, and to praise
you by the kind of life I live, as well as by my
lips. I long to give glory, honor and thanks to
you always.

May your indwelling Spirit—the Spirit of
glory—ever keep before me the great privilege
of being an heir of your glory, and a citizen of
heaven. May my life in its praise and worship
of you now be the closest possible approximation
to the praise and worship of heaven.

Father, I worship and adore you, through
Jesus Christ your Son.
Amen.

DEREK PRIME

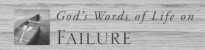

David said to Solomon his son, "Be strong and courageous, and do the work. Do not be afraid or discouraged, for the LORD God, my God, is with you. He will not fail you or forsake you."

1 CHRONICLES 28:20

Because of the LORD's great love
we are not consumed,
for his compassions never fail.
They are new every morning;
great is your faithfulness.

LAMENTATIONS 3:22–23

[God] will remain faithful, for he cannot disown himself.

2 TIMOTHY 2:13

We do not have a high priest who is unable to sympathize with our weaknesses, but we have one who has been tempted in every way, just as we are—yet was without sin. Let us then approach the throne of grace with confidence, so that we may receive mercy and find grace to help us in our time of need.

HEBREWS 4:15–16

[God] said to me, "My grace is sufficient for you, for my power is made perfect in weakness." Therefore I will boast all the more gladly about my weaknesses, so that Christ's power may rest on me.

2 CORINTHIANS 12:9

The LORD is good,
  a refuge in times of trouble.
He cares for those who trust in him.

       NAHUM 1:7

When you pass through the waters,
  I will be with you;
and when you pass through the rivers,
  they will not sweep over you.
When you walk through the fire,
  you will not be burned;
  the flames will not set you ablaze.

       ISAIAH 43:2

Though I walk in the midst of trouble,
  you preserve my life;
you stretch out your hand against the
    anger of my foes,
  with your right hand you save me.

       PSALM 138:7

Praise be to the God and Father of our Lord Jesus
Christ, the Father of compassion and the God of
all comfort, who comforts us in all our troubles,
so that we can comfort those in any trouble with
the comfort we ourselves have received from God.

    2 CORINTHIANS 1:3–4

Everything that was written in the past was
written to teach us, so that through endurance
and the encouragement of the Scriptures we
might have hope.

      ROMANS 15:4

We know that in all things God works for the good of those who love him, who have been called according to his purpose.

ROMANS 8:28

I lift up my eyes to the hills—
    where does my help come from?
My help comes from the LORD,
    the Maker of heaven and earth.

PSALM 121:1–2

Do not conform any longer to the pattern of this world, but be transformed by the renewing of your mind. Then you will be able to test and approve what God's will is—his good, pleasing and perfect will.

ROMANS 12:2

All this is for your benefit, so that the grace that is reaching more and more people may cause thanksgiving to overflow to the glory of God. Therefore we do not lose heart. Though outwardly we are wasting away, yet inwardly we are being renewed day by day. For our light and momentary troubles are achieving for us an eternal glory that far outweighs them all. So we fix our eyes not on what is seen, but on what is unseen. For what is seen is temporary, but what is unseen is eternal.

2 CORINTHIANS 4:15–18

It would be a tragedy if my kids grew up knowing only that their dad was a good football player and husband and father. If they thought I expected them to live every minute of their lives the way they have seen me live as they grew up, they would be frustrated and devastated if they ever failed. I want them to know what they didn't see, when I failed miserably and only came out of it by the grace of God.

As they get older and able to understand, I'm committed to being open and honest with them. I want them to know of my mistakes so they can avoid them. I also want them to know of my mistakes because they will make their own, and I don't want them to feel they are the first person in the family to fail.

I want to be able to sit with my kids and tell them some of the things I have done. Not to glorify sin. Not to justify it. Not to say everybody does it so it must be okay. Rather, because I'm not proud of it and because I don't want them to feel unique. Most of all, I want them to know that by the grace of God, he brought me through it and out of it, and he can do the same for them.

MIKE SINGLETARY

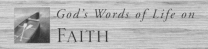

Make every effort to add to your faith goodness; and to goodness, knowledge; and to knowledge, self-control; and to self-control, perseverance; and to perseverance, godliness; and to godliness, brotherly kindness; and to brotherly kindness, love. For if you possess these qualities in increasing measure, they will keep you from being ineffective and unproductive in your knowledge of our Lord Jesus Christ.

2 PETER 1:5–8

Abram believed the LORD, and he credited it to him as righteousness.

GENESIS 15:6

Faith comes from hearing the message, and the message is heard through the word of Christ.

ROMANS 10:17

Do not think of yourself more highly than you ought, but rather think of yourself with sober judgment, in accordance with the measure of faith God has given you.

ROMANS 12:3

"Have faith in God," Jesus answered. "I tell you the truth, if anyone says to this mountain, 'Go, throw yourself into the sea,' and does not doubt in his heart but believes that what he says will happen, it will be done for him. Therefore I tell you, whatever you ask for in prayer, believe that you have received it, and it will be yours."

MARK 11:22–24

Let us fix our eyes on Jesus, the author and perfecter of our faith, who for the joy set before him endured the cross, scorning its shame, and sat down at the right hand of the throne of God.

HEBREWS 12:2

Jesus replied, "Because you have so little faith. I tell you the truth, if you have faith as small as a mustard seed, you can say to this mountain, 'Move from here to there' and it will move. Nothing will be impossible for you."

MATTHEW 17:20

In the gospel a righteousness from God is revealed, a righteousness that is by faith from first to last, just as it is written: "The righteous will live by faith."

ROMANS 1:17

We live by faith, not by sight.

2 CORINTHIANS 5:7

Without faith it is impossible to please God, because anyone who comes to him must believe that he exists and that he rewards those who earnestly seek him.

HEBREWS 11:6

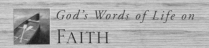
These have come so that your faith—of greater
worth than gold, which perishes even though
refined by fire—may be proved genuine and may
result in praise, glory and honor when Jesus Christ
is revealed. Though you have not seen him, you
love him; and even though you do not see him
now, you believe in him and are filled with an
inexpressible and glorious joy, for you are receiving
the goal of your faith, the salvation of your souls.

1 PETER 1:7–9

Just then a woman . . . came up behind him and
touched the edge of his cloak. She said to herself,
"If I only touch his cloak, I will be healed." Jesus
turned and saw her. "Take heart, daughter," he
said, "your faith has healed you." And the woman
was healed from that moment.

MATTHEW 9:20–22

Jesus said, "According to your faith will it be
done to you."

MATTHEW 9:29

Faith is being sure of what we hope for and
certain of what we do not see.

HEBREWS 11:1

Jesus said, "I tell you the truth, anyone who has faith in me will do what I have been doing. He will do even greater things than these, because I am going to the Father. And I will do whatever you ask in my name, so that the Son may bring glory to the Father. You may ask me for anything in my name, and I will do it."

JOHN 14:12–14

To the man who does not work but trusts God who justifies the wicked, his faith is credited as righteousness.

ROMANS 4:5

Since we have been justified through faith, we have peace with God through our Lord Jesus Christ, through whom we have gained access by faith into this grace in which we now stand. And we rejoice in the hope of the glory of God.

ROMANS 5:1–2

Be on your guard; stand firm in the faith; be men of courage; be strong.

1 CORINTHIANS 16:13

I have been crucified with Christ and I no longer live, but Christ lives in me. The life I live in the body, I live by faith in the Son of God, who loved me and gave himself for me.

GALATIANS 2:20

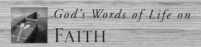

It is by grace you have been saved, through
faith—and this not from yourselves, it is the gift
of God—not by works, so that no one can boast.

EPHESIANS 2:8–9

Though I am absent from you in body, I am
present with you in spirit and delight to see how
orderly you are and how firm your faith in Christ
is. So then, just as you received Christ Jesus as
Lord, continue to live in him, rooted and built
up in him, strengthened in the faith as you were
taught, and overflowing with thankfulness.

COLOSSIANS 2:5–7

God was perfect and I wasn't. I was just a guy, and he was, well, God. How could I relate to him? A friend named Butch said Jesus was the answer. I could relate to him because even though he was perfect, he had also become a man. He was the bridge. He paid for my sin. If I could accept that and believe in Christ, then I could be forgiven and know I was going to heaven.

Overnight I pulled out the Gideon Bible. My mind was racing. Do I believe in God? Yes. Do I believe the Bible is God's message to man? Yes. Do I believe what the Bible says? Yes. That all have sinned? Yes. Do I want to become a Christian? How does one go about praying? I didn't know. I figured if God was God, he would understand if I just told him what was on my mind.

I said, "God, I don't know everything about you. But I know I'm a sinner and I know I want to be forgiven. I know I want Christ in my life, and I want to go to heaven. I want to become a Christian. With that, I accept you. Amen." No tears, no lightning, no wind. What a relief! I knew I had done the right thing. I had stepped from skepticism to belief.

 OREL HERSHISER

[God] passed in front of Moses, proclaiming, "The LORD, the LORD, the compassionate and gracious God, slow to anger, abounding in love and faithfulness."

EXODUS 34:6

Your love, O LORD, reaches to the heavens,
your faithfulness to the skies.

PSALM 36:5

God sends his love and his faithfulness.
I will praise you, O LORD, among the nations;
I will sing of you among the peoples.
For great is your love, reaching to the heavens;
your faithfulness reaches to the skies.

PSALM 57:3, 9–10

I put in charge of Jerusalem my brother Hanani, along with Hananiah the commander of the citadel, because he was a man of integrity and feared God more than most men do.

NEHEMIAH 7:2

Jesus said, "Who then is the faithful and wise servant, whom the master has put in charge of the servants in his household to give them their food at the proper time? It will be good for that servant whose master finds him doing so when he returns. I tell you the truth, he will put him in charge of all his possessions."

MATTHEW 24:45–47

[God] will cover you with his feathers,
and under his wings you will find refuge;
his faithfulness will be your
shield and rampart.

PSALM 91:4

The LORD is good and his love endures forever;
his faithfulness continues
through all generations.

PSALM 100:5

My eyes will be on the faithful in the land,
that they may dwell with me;
he whose walk is blameless
will minister to me.

PSALM 101:6–7

It is required that those who have been given a
trust must prove faithful.

1 CORINTHIANS 4:2

They could find no corruption in Daniel,
because he was trustworthy and neither corrupt
nor negligent.

DANIEL 6:4

Let love and faithfulness never leave you;
bind them around your neck,
write them on the tablet of your heart.
Then you will win favor and a good name
in the sight of God and man.

PROVERBS 3:3–4

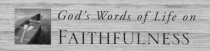
His master replied, "Well done, good and faithful servant! You have been faithful with a few things; I will put you in charge of many things. Come and share your master's happiness!"

MATTHEW 25:21

The fruit of the Spirit is love, joy, peace, patience, kindness, goodness, faithfulness, gentleness and self-control.

GALATIANS 5:22–23

A faithful man will be richly blessed,
but one eager to get rich will
not go unpunished.

PROVERBS 28:20

I have kept the ways of the LORD;
I have not done evil by turning from my God.
All his laws are before me;
I have not turned away from his decrees.
I have been blameless before him
and have kept myself from sin.
The Lord has rewarded me according
to my righteousness,
according to my cleanness in his sight.
To the faithful you show yourself faithful,
to the blameless you show yourself blameless.

2 SAMUEL 22:22–26

Yet this I call to mind
and therefore I have hope:
Because of the LORD's great love we are not consumed,
for his compassions never fail.
They are new every morning;
great is your faithfulness.

LAMENTATIONS 3:21–23

B iblical friendship calls for faithfulness. Circumstances should not affect our consistency. In Romans 12:15 Paul tells us to "rejoice with those who rejoice; mourn with those who mourn."

Faithfulness is critical to a close relationship because we depend on those who are close to us. Christ's deepest hurts occurred within his circle of closest companions, and David was wounded emotionally more by the treachery of his close friends than by the efforts of his enemies (Psalm 55:12–14). Paul too was left to stand alone when he was deserted by Demas and others (2 Timothy 4:10).

A faithful friend keeps confidences. In Proverbs we read that "a perverse man stirs up dissension, and a gossip separates close friends" (16:28). Entering friendship involves revealing yourself in confidence to another, and thus becoming vulnerable. This is as it should be, but it is what makes betrayal so evil and faithfulness so virtuous.

DAVID W. SMITH

The LORD is my shepherd, I shall not be in want.
PSALM 23:1

Jesus said, "No one can serve two masters. Either he will hate the one and love the other, or he will be devoted to the one and despise the other. You cannot serve both God and Money."
MATTHEW 6:24

Whoever trusts in his riches will fall,
but the righteous will thrive like a green leaf.
PROVERBS 11:28

Godliness with contentment is great gain. For we brought nothing into the world, and we can take nothing out of it. But if we have food and clothing, we will be content with that. People who want to get rich fall into temptation and a trap and into many foolish and harmful desires that plunge men into ruin and destruction. For the love of money is a root of all kinds of evil. Some people, eager for money, have wandered from the faith and pierced themselves with many griefs.
1 TIMOTHY 6:6–10

I know what it is to be in need, and I know what it is to have plenty. I have learned the secret of being content in any and every situation, whether well fed or hungry, whether living in plenty or in want.
PHILIPPIANS 4:12

Jesus sat down opposite the place where the
offerings were put and watched the crowd putting
their money into the temple treasury. Many rich
people threw in large amounts. But a poor widow
came and put in two very small copper coins,
worth only a fraction of a penny. Calling his
disciples to him, Jesus said, "I tell you the truth,
this poor widow has put more into the treasury
than all the others. They all gave out of their
wealth; but she, out of her poverty, put in
everything—all she had to live on."

MARK 12:41–44

"Will a man rob God? Yet you rob me. But you
ask, 'How do we rob you?' In tithes and offerings.
You are under a curse—the whole nation of you—
because you are robbing me. Bring the whole tithe
into the storehouse, that there may be food in my
house. Test me in this," says the LORD Almighty,
"and see if I will not throw open the floodgates of
heaven and pour out so much blessing that you
will not have room enough for it."

MALACHI 3:8–10

Then Jesus said to them, "Watch out! Be on your
guard against all kinds of greed; a man's life does
not consist in the abundance of his possessions."

LUKE 12:15

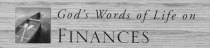
Keep your lives free from the love of money and be content with what you have, because God has said, "Never will I leave you; never will I forsake you."

HEBREWS 13:5

Make it your ambition to lead a quiet life, to mind your own business and to work with your hands, just as we told you, so that your daily life may win the respect of outsiders and so that you will not be dependent on anybody.

1 THESSALONIANS 4:11–12

Jesus said, "Do not worry, saying, 'What shall we eat?' or 'What shall we drink?' or 'What shall we wear?' For the pagans run after all these things, and your heavenly Father knows that you need them. But seek first his kingdom and his righteousness, and all these things will be given to you as well.

MATTHEW 6:31–33

Let no debt remain outstanding, except the continuing debt to love one another, for he who loves his fellowman has fulfilled the law.

ROMANS 13:8

Do not let this Book of the Law depart from your mouth; meditate on it day and night, so that you may be careful to do everything written in it. Then you will be prosperous and successful.

JOSHUA 1:8

A good man leaves an inheritance for
his children's children,
but a sinner's wealth is stored up
for the righteous.

PROVERBS 13:22

Remember the LORD your God, for it is he who gives you the ability to produce wealth, and so confirms his covenant, which he swore to your forefathers, as it is today.

DEUTERONOMY 8:18

My God will meet all your needs according to his glorious riches in Christ Jesus.

PHILIPPIANS 4:19

Jesus looked at him and loved him. "One thing you lack," he said. "Go, sell everything you have and give to the poor, and you will have treasure in heaven. Then come, follow me." At this the man's face fell. He went away sad, because he had great wealth.

MARK 10:21–22

God is able to make all grace abound to you, so that in all things at all times, having all that you need, you will abound in every good work.

2 CORINTHIANS 9:8

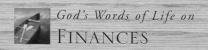
Jesus said, "Store up for yourselves treasures in heaven, where moth and rust do not destroy, and where thieves do not break in and steal. For where your treasure is, there your heart will be also."

MATTHEW 6:20–21

If they obey and serve God,
they will spend the rest of
their days in prosperity
and their years in contentment.

JOB 36:11

Jesus said, "Give, and it will be given to you. A good measure, pressed down, shaken together and running over, will be poured into your lap. For with the measure you use, it will be measured to you."

LUKE 6:38

Never settle for second-rate or selfish goals. Set goals for yourself that involve helping other people and the riches will follow.

The richest people I know are those who have given themselves unselfishly to other people. Such motivation will affect the way you sell, cook, teach or ply your particular trade.

True riches, of course, are totally unrelated to money or material reward. In fact, if a person has earned money without helping people, his money will not buy him happiness.

Of one thing I am sure: happy people have strong goals—and somehow these include helping other people. They can also be assured that they will never run out of people to help.

TIM LAHAYE

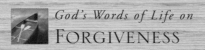
You forgave the iniquity of your people
and covered all their sins.

PSALM 85:2

As far as the east is from the west,
so far has God removed our
transgressions from us.

PSALM 103:12

If anybody does sin, we have one who speaks to
the Father in our defense—Jesus Christ, the
Righteous One.

1 JOHN 2:1

If we confess our sins, [God] is faithful and just
and will forgive us our sins and purify us from all
unrighteousness.

1 JOHN 1:9

Jesus said, "When you stand praying, if you hold
anything against anyone, forgive him, so that
your Father in heaven may forgive you your sins."

MARK 11:25

Forgive whatever grievances you may have against
one another. Forgive as the Lord forgave you.

COLOSSIANS 3:13

The LORD said, "I will cleanse them from all the sin they have committed against me and will forgive all their sins of rebellion against me."

JEREMIAH 33:8

"Come now, let us reason together,"
says the LORD.
"Though your sins are like scarlet,
they shall be as white as snow;
though they are red as crimson,
they shall be like wool."

ISAIAH 1:18

When you were dead in your sins and in the uncircumcision of your sinful nature, God made you alive with Christ. He forgave us all our sins.

COLOSSIANS 2:13

"I, even I, am he who blots out
your transgressions, for my own sake,
and remembers your sins no
more," says the LORD.

ISAIAH 43:25

In him we have redemption through his blood, the forgiveness of sins, in accordance with the riches of God's grace.

EPHESIANS 1:7

Blessed is he
whose transgressions are forgiven,
whose sins are covered.
Blessed is the man
whose sin the LORD does not count against him
and in whose spirit is no deceit.

PSALM 32:1–2

Jesus said, "I tell you the truth, all the sins and blasphemies of men will be forgiven them."

MARK 3:28

Let the wicked forsake his way
and the evil man his thoughts.
Let him turn to the LORD, and
he will have mercy on him,
and to our God, for he will freely pardon.
ISAIAH 55:7

Once you were alienated from God and were enemies in your minds because of your evil behavior. But now he has reconciled you by Christ's physical body through death to present you holy in God's sight, without blemish and free from accusation.

COLOSSIANS 1:21–22

Blessed are they whose transgressions are forgiven,
whose sins are covered.
ROMANS 4:7

The LORD said, "If my people, who are called by my name, will humble themselves and pray and seek my face and turn from their wicked ways, then will I hear from heaven and will forgive their sin and will heal their land."

2 CHRONICLES 7:14

"I will forgive their wickedness and will remember
their sins no more," says the Lord.
HEBREWS 8:12

Peter came to Jesus and asked, "Lord, how many times shall I forgive my brother when he sins against me? Up to seven times?" Jesus answered, "I tell you, not seven times, but seventy-seven times."

MATTHEW 18:21–22

> O Lord, hear my voice.
> Let your ears be attentive
>   to my cry for mercy.
> If you, O LORD, kept a record of sins,
>   O Lord, who could stand?
> But with you there is forgiveness;
>   therefore you are feared.
> I wait for the LORD, my soul waits,
>   and in his word I put my hope.

PSALM 130:2–5

Peter replied, "Repent and be baptized, every one of you, in the name of Jesus Christ for the forgiveness of your sins. And you will receive the gift of the Holy Spirit. The promise is for you and your children and for all who are far off—for all whom the Lord our God will call."

ACTS 2:38–39

> Help us, O God our Savior,
>   for the glory of your name;
> deliver us and forgive our sins
>   for your name's sake.

PSALM 79:9

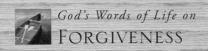
Jesus said, "If you forgive men when they sin against you, your heavenly Father will also forgive you. But if you do not forgive men their sins, your Father will not forgive your sins."

MATTHEW 6:14–15

Jesus said, "Do not judge, and you will not be judged. Do not condemn, and you will not be condemned. Forgive, and you will be forgiven. Give, and it will be given to you. A good measure, pressed down, shaken together and running over, will be poured into your lap. For with the measure you use, it will be measured to you."

LUKE 6:37–38

Be kind and compassionate to one another, forgiving each other, just as in Christ God forgave you.

EPHESIANS 4:32

Forgiving is love's revolution against love's unfairness. When we forgive, we ignore the normal laws that strap us to the natural law of getting even and, by the alchemy of love, we release ourselves from our own painful pasts.

We fly over a dues-paying morality in order to create a new future out of the past's unfairness. We free ourselves from the wrong that is locked into our private histories.

We unshackle our spirits from malice; and, maybe, if we are lucky, we also restore a relationship that would otherwise be lost forever.

LEWIS B. SMEDES

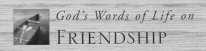
A friend loves at all times,
and a brother is born for adversity.

PROVERBS 17:17

Jesus said, "I no longer call you servants, because
a servant does not know his master's business.
Instead, I have called you friends, for everything
that I learned from my Father I have made
known to you."

JOHN 15:15

A despairing man should have
the devotion of his friends,
even though he forsakes the
fear of the Almighty.

JOB 6:14

My intercessor is my friend
as my eyes pour out tears to God.

JOB 16:20

He who covers over an offense
promotes love,
but whoever repeats the
matter separates close friends.

PROVERBS 17:9

A man of many companions
may come to ruin,
but there is a friend who
sticks closer than a brother.

PROVERBS 18:24

Two are better than one,
　　because they have a good return for their work:
If one falls down,
　　his friend can help him up.
But pity the man who falls
　　and has no one to help him up!

ECCLESIASTES 4:9–10

Do not make friends with a hot-tempered man,
　　do not associate with one easily angered,
or you may learn his ways
　　and get yourself ensnared.

PROVERBS 22:24–25

Wounds from a friend can be trusted.

PROVERBS 27:6

Jesus said, "Greater love has no one than this,
that he lay down his life for his friends. You are
my friends if you do what I command."

JOHN 15:13–14

Perfume and incense bring joy
　　　　to the heart,
　　and the pleasantness of
　　　　　　one's friend springs from
　　　　　　his earnest counsel.

PROVERBS 27:9

If two lie down together, they will keep warm.
　　But how can one keep warm alone?
Though one may be overpowered,
　　two can defend themselves.
A cord of three strands is not
　　　　quickly broken.

ECCLESIASTES 4:11–12

The LORD would speak to Moses face to face, as a man speaks with his friend.

EXODUS 33:11

He who loves a pure heart and
whose speech is gracious
will have the king for his friend.

PROVERBS 22:11

A righteous man is cautious in friendship,
but the way of the wicked
leads them astray.

PROVERBS 12:26

A perverse man stirs up dissension,
and a gossip separates close friends.

PROVERBS 16:28

Jonathan had David reaffirm his oath out of love for him, because he loved him as he loved himself.

1 SAMUEL 20:17

One of the finest examples of male friendship is found in the historical record of 1 Samuel. Here we read about real male friendship, about a relationship that ran deep between Jonathan, the king's son, and David, a shepherd boy and God's future choice for the throne. Their friendship was strong, built solidly on an inward attachment rather than on an outer attraction or social status. These men demonstrated a mutual acceptance of each other despite their different social backgrounds. David's interests were more important to Jonathan than his own, and David felt the same way about Jonathan's interests.

If you study the friendship between David and Jonathan, you will walk away with a good understanding of what a healthy friendship between men can and should be. Any definition should include the following: unconditional love, personal enjoyment, mutual acceptance, mutual interests, mutual commitment, and mutual loyalty.

In short, friendship involves a concern for and involvement with the well-being of another.

DAVID W. SMITH

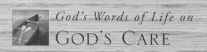
Jesus said, "I will give you words and wisdom that none of your adversaries will be able to resist or contradict."

LUKE 21:15

Every good and perfect gift is from above, coming down from the Father of the heavenly lights, who does not change like shifting shadows.

JAMES 1:17

[God] said to me, "My grace is sufficient for you, for my power is made perfect in weakness." Therefore I will boast all the more gladly about my weaknesses, so that Christ's power may rest on me.

2 CORINTHIANS 12:9

It is God who works in you to will and to act according to his good purpose.

PHILIPPIANS 2:13

I can do everything through him who gives me strength.

PHILIPPIANS 4:13

"This is the covenant I will
make with the house of Israel
after that time," declares the LORD.
"I will put my law in their minds
and write it on their hearts.
I will be their God,
and they will be my people."

JEREMIAH 31:33

Not that we are competent in ourselves to claim anything for ourselves, but our competence comes from God.

2 CORINTHIANS 3:5

Jesus said, "If you remain in me and my words remain in you, ask whatever you wish, and it will be given you."

JOHN 15:7

Praise be to the God and Father of our Lord Jesus Christ, who has blessed us in the heavenly realms with every spiritual blessing in Christ.

EPHESIANS 1:3

He who did not spare his own Son, but gave him up for us all—how will he not also, along with him, graciously give us all things?

ROMANS 8:32

Praise the LORD, O my soul,
and forget not all his benefits—
who forgives all your sins
and heals all your diseases,
who redeems your life from the pit
and crowns you with love and compassion,
who satisfies your desires with good things
so that your youth is renewed like the eagle's.

PSALM 103:2–5

Delight yourself in the LORD
and he will give you the
desires of your heart.

PSALM 37:4

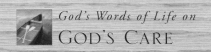

Jesus said, "Whoever drinks the water I give him will never thirst. Indeed, the water I give him will become in him a spring of water welling up to eternal life."

JOHN 4:14

The eyes of all look to you, O LORD,
*   and you give them their food at the proper time.*
You open your hand
*   and satisfy the desires of every living thing.*

PSALM 145:15–16

Praise be to the LORD, to God our Savior,
*   who daily bears our burdens.*

PSALM 68:19

Remember how the LORD your God led you all the way in the desert these forty years, to humble you and to test you in order to know what was in your heart, whether or not you would keep his commands.

DEUTERONOMY 8:2

The eyes of the LORD range throughout the earth to strengthen those whose hearts are fully committed to him.

2 CHRONICLES 16:9

Jesus said, "Are not two sparrows sold for a penny? Yet not one of them will fall to the ground apart from the will of your Father. And even the very hairs of your head are all numbered. So don't be afraid; you are worth more than many sparrows."

MATTHEW 10:29–31

You are a shield around me, O LORD;
you bestow glory on me and lift up my head.

PSALM 3:3

I love the LORD, for he heard my voice;
he heard my cry for mercy.

PSALM 116:1

The LORD is my shepherd, I shall not be in want.
He makes me lie down in green pastures,
he leads me beside quiet waters,
he restores my soul.
He guides me in paths of righteousness
for his name's sake.

PSALM 23:1–3

Because of the LORD's great
love we are not consumed,
for his compassions never fail.
They are new every morning;
great is your faithfulness.
I say to myself, "The LORD is my portion;
therefore I will wait for him."
The LORD is good to those whose hope is in him,
to the one who seeks him;
it is good to wait quietly
for the salvation of the LORD.

LAMENTATIONS 3:22-26

O LORD, you have searched me
  and you know me.
You know when I sit and when I rise;
  you perceive my thoughts from afar.
You discern my going out and my lying down;
  you are familiar with all my ways.
You hem me in—behind and before;
  you have laid your hand upon me.
Where can I go from your Spirit?
  Where can I flee from your presence?
If I go up to the heavens, you are there;
  if I make my bed in the depths, you are there.
If I rise on the wings of the dawn,
  if I settle on the far side of the sea,
even there your hand will guide me,
  your right hand will hold me fast.
For you created my inmost being;
  you knit me together in my mother's womb.
My frame was not hidden from you
  when I was made in the secret place.
When I was woven together in the depths of the earth,
  your eyes saw my unformed body.
All the days ordained for me
  were written in your book
  before one of them came to be.

PSALM 139:1–3, 5, 7–10, 13, 15–16

I am progressing along the path of life in my ordinary contentedly fallen and godless condition, absorbed in a merry meeting with my friends for the morrow or a bit of work that tickles my vanity today, a holiday or a new book, when suddenly a stab of abdominal pain that threatens serious disease, or a headline in the newspapers that threatens us all with destruction, sends this whole pack of cards tumbling down.

At first I am overwhelmed, and all my little happinesses look like broken toys. Then, slowly and reluctantly, bit by bit, I try to bring myself into the frame of mind that I should be in at all times.

I remind myself that all these toys were never intended to possess my heart, that my true good is in another world and my only real treasure is Christ. Perhaps, by God's grace, I succeed, and for a day or two become a creature consciously dependent on God and drawing its strength from the right sources.

But the moment the threat is withdrawn, my whole nature leaps back to the toys....The terrible necessity of tribulation is only too clear ...my only real treasure must be Christ.

C. S. LEWIS

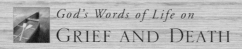
If only for this life we have hope in Christ, we are
to be pitied more than all men. But Christ has
indeed been raised from the dead, the firstfruits
of those who have fallen asleep. For since death
came through a man, the resurrection of the dead
comes also through a man. For as in Adam all
die, so in Christ all will be made alive.

1 CORINTHIANS 15:19–22

Listen, I tell you a mystery: We will not all sleep,
but we will all be changed—in a flash, in the
twinkling of an eye, at the last trumpet. For the
trumpet will sound, the dead will be raised
imperishable, and we will be changed. For the
perishable must clothe itself with the imperishable,
and the mortal with immortality. When the
perishable has been clothed with the imperishable,
and the mortal with immortality, then the saying
that is written will come true: "Death has been
swallowed up in victory." "Where, O death, is your
victory? Where, O death, is your sting?"

1 CORINTHIANS 15:51–55

Even though I walk
through the valley of the shadow of death,
I will fear no evil,
for you are with me;
your rod and your staff,
they comfort me.

PSALM 23:4

We believe that Jesus died and rose again and so we believe that God will bring with Jesus those who have fallen asleep in him. According to the Lord's own word, we tell you that we who are still alive, who are left till the coming of the Lord, will certainly not precede those who have fallen asleep. For the Lord himself will come down from heaven, with a loud command, with the voice of the archangel and with the trumpet call of God, and the dead in Christ will rise first. After that, we who are still alive and are left will be caught up together with them in the clouds to meet the Lord in the air. And so we will be with the Lord forever.

1 THESSALONIANS 4:14–18

The LORD brings death and makes alive;
*   he brings down to the grave and raises up.*

1 SAMUEL 2:6

I heard a loud voice from the throne saying, "Now the dwelling of God is with men, and he will live with them. They will be his people, and God himself will be with them and be their God. He will wipe every tear from their eyes. There will be no more death or mourning or crying or pain, for the old order of things has passed away."

REVELATION 21:3–4

Into your hands I commit my spirit;
*   redeem me, O LORD, the God of truth.*

PSALM 31:5

You guide me with your counsel,
and afterward you will take me into glory.
Whom have I in heaven but you?
And earth has nothing I desire besides you.
My flesh and my heart may fail,
but God is the strength of my heart
and my portion forever.

PSALM 73:24–26

Precious in the sight of the LORD
is the death of his saints.

PSALM 116:15

Those who walk uprightly
enter into peace;
they find rest as they lie in death.

ISAIAH 57:2

None of us lives to himself alone and none of us
dies to himself alone. If we live, we live to the
Lord; and if we die, we die to the Lord. So,
whether we live or die, we belong to the Lord.

ROMANS 14:7–8

We know that if the earthly tent we live in is
destroyed, we have a building from God, an eternal
house in heaven, not built by human hands.

2 CORINTHIANS 5:1

[Christ] died for us so that, whether we are awake
or asleep, we may live together with him.

1 THESSALONIANS 5:10

To live is Christ and to die is gain.

PHILIPPIANS 1:21

There is in store for me the crown of righteousness, which the Lord, the righteous Judge, will award to me on that day—and not only to me, but also to all who have longed for his appearing.

2 TIMOTHY 4:8

Since the children have flesh and blood, he too shared in their humanity so that by his death he might destroy him who holds the power of death—that is, the devil—and free those who all their lives were held in slavery by their fear of death.

HEBREWS 2:14–15

I heard a voice from heaven say, "Blessed are the dead who die in the Lord from now on." "Yes," says the Spirit, "they will rest from their labor, for their deeds will follow them."

REVELATION 14:13

If Christ is in you, your body is dead because of sin, yet your spirit is alive because of righteousness. And if the Spirit of him who raised Jesus from the dead is living in you, he who raised Christ from the dead will also give life to your mortal bodies through his Spirit, who lives in you.

ROMANS 8:10–11

My comfort in my suffering is this:
Your promise preserves my life.

PSALM 119:50

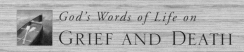

Jesus said, "Blessed are those who mourn,
for they will be comforted."
MATTHEW 5:4

The eyes of the LORD are on those who fear him,
on those whose hope is in his unfailing love,
to deliver them from death
and keep them alive in famine.
We wait in hope for the LORD;
he is our help and our shield.
In him our hearts rejoice,
for we trust in his holy name.
May your unfailing love rest
upon us, O LORD,
even as we put our hope in you.
PSALM 33:18–22

He will swallow up death forever.
The Sovereign LORD will wipe away the tears
from all faces;
he will remove the disgrace of his people
from all the earth.
The LORD has spoken.
ISAIAH 25:8

I am convinced that neither death nor life,
neither angels nor demons, neither the present
nor the future, nor any powers, neither height
nor depth, nor anything else in all creation, will
be able to separate us from the love of God that is
in Christ Jesus our Lord.
ROMANS 8:38–39

How much faith is enough in our mourning? Some of us feel that it is always more than what we have.

Jesus said that the amount of faith isn't important. If we have faith, though it be as small as a mustard seed, nothing will be impossible.

I interpret faith in this instance as basic trust. We don't need a huge quantity of it in order to get on with our bereavement. In fact, if we worry about having a lot of faith, we may miss the mustard seed we do have.

The giver of this grain of faith is God, whose Son maintained his faith. He went through his Gethsemane of grief with the word "Father" still on his lips.

We too can go through the valleys and mountains of our bereavement journey with "Father" on our lips. Our hearts may wonder, doubt and cry out in pain, but these feelings will not obliterate our faith. Even when we think we have lost that mustard seed, we do well to remember that our Father is faithful, for he has loved us first.

PHILIP W. WILLIAMS

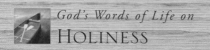
It is the LORD your God you must follow, and
him you must revere. Keep his commands and
obey him; serve him and hold fast to him.

DEUTERONOMY 13:4

I urge you, brothers, in view of God's mercy, to
offer your bodies as living sacrifices, holy and
pleasing to God—this is your spiritual act of
worship. Do not conform any longer to the
pattern of this world, but be transformed by the
renewing of your mind. Then you will be able to
test and approve what God's will is—his good,
pleasing and perfect will.

ROMANS 12:1–2

Make every effort to live in peace with all men
and to be holy; without holiness no one will see
the Lord.

HEBREWS 12:14

God did not call us to be impure, but to live a
holy life.

1 THESSALONIANS 4:7

What does the LORD your God ask of you but to
fear the LORD your God, to walk in all his ways,
to love him, to serve the LORD your God with all
your heart and with all your soul.

DEUTERONOMY 10:12

Serve God with wholehearted devotion and with a willing mind, for the LORD searches every heart and understands every motive behind the thoughts. If you seek him, he will be found by you; but if you forsake him, he will reject you forever.

1 CHRONICLES 28:9

By dying to what once bound us, we have been released from the law so that we serve in the new way of the Spirit, and not in the old way of the written code.

ROMANS 7:6

Samuel replied:
"Does the LORD delight in
burnt offerings and sacrifices
as much as in obeying the voice of the LORD?
To obey is better than sacrifice,
and to heed is better than the fat of rams."

1 SAMUEL 15:22

If only you had paid attention to my commands,
your peace would have been like a river,
your righteousness like the waves of the sea.

ISAIAH 48:18

Obey me, and I will be your God and you will be my people. Walk in all the ways I command you, that it may go well with you.

JEREMIAH 7:23

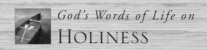
Be very careful to keep the commandment and
the law that Moses the servant of the LORD gave
you: to love the LORD your God, to walk in all
his ways, to obey his commands, to hold fast to
him and to serve him with all your heart and all
your soul.

JOSHUA 22:5

Now that you have been set free from sin and
have become slaves to God, the benefit you reap
leads to holiness, and the result is eternal life.

ROMANS 6:22

Since we have these promises, dear friends, let us
purify ourselves from everything that
contaminates body and spirit, perfecting holiness
out of reverence for God.

2 CORINTHIANS 7:1

Our people must learn to devote themselves to
doing what is good, in order that they may
provide for daily necessities and not live
unproductive lives.

TITUS 3:14

[God] has raised up a horn of salvation for us
in the house of his servant David ...
to rescue us from the hand of our enemies,
and to enable us to serve him without fear
in holiness and righteousness before him
all our days.

LUKE 1:69, 74–75

May [God] strengthen your hearts so that you will be blameless and holy in the presence of our God and Father when our Lord Jesus comes with all his holy ones.

1 THESSALONIANS 3:13

Just as he who called you is holy, so be holy in all you do; for it is written: "Be holy, because I am holy."

1 PETER 1:15–16

Since we have confidence to enter the Most Holy Place by the blood of Jesus, by a new and living way opened for us through the curtain, that is, his body, and since we have a great priest over the house of God, let us draw near to God with a sincere heart in full assurance of faith, having our hearts sprinkled to cleanse us from a guilty conscience and having our bodies washed with pure water. Let us hold unswervingly to the hope we profess, for he who promised is faithful. And let us consider how we may spur one another on toward love and good deeds. Let us not give up meeting together, as some are in the habit of doing, but let us encourage one another—and all the more as you see the Day approaching.

HEBREWS 10:19–25

Since we are receiving a kingdom that cannot be shaken, let us be thankful, and so worship God acceptably with reverence and awe, for our "God is a consuming fire."

HEBREWS 12:28–29

Ascribe to the LORD, O families of nations,
ascribe to the LORD glory and strength,
ascribe to the LORD the glory due his name.
Bring an offering and come before him;
worship the LORD in the
splendor of his holiness.

1 CHRONICLES 16:28–29

I will show my greatness and my holiness, and I will make myself known in the sight of many nations. Then they will know that I am the LORD.

EZEKIEL 38:23

Our fathers disciplined us for a little while as they thought best; but God disciplines us for our good, that we may share in his holiness.

HEBREWS 12:10

It is because of him that you are in Christ Jesus, who has become for us wisdom from God—that is, our righteousness, holiness and redemption.

1 CORINTHIANS 1:30

O ne of the more serious sins of Christians today may well be the almost flippant familiarity with which we often address God in prayer. None of the godly men of the Bible ever adopted the casual manner we often do.

In our day we must begin to recover a sense of awe and profound reverence for God. We must begin to view him once again in the infinite majesty that alone belongs to him who is the Creator and Supreme Ruler of the entire universe. There is an infinite gap in worth and dignity between God the Creator and man the creature, even though man has been created in the image of God. The fear of God is a heartfelt recognition of this gap—not a put-down of man, but an exaltation of God.

We seem to have magnified the love of God almost to the exclusion of the fear of God. Because of this preoccupation we are not honoring God and reverencing him as we should. We should magnify the love of God; but although we revel in his love and mercy, we must never lose sight of his majesty and his holiness.

JERRY BRIDGES

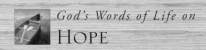

Be strong and take heart,
all you who hope in the LORD.

PSALM 31:24

The eyes of the LORD are on those who fear him,
on those whose hope is in his unfailing love.

PSALM 33:18

May your unfailing love rest upon us, O LORD,
even as we put our hope in you.

PSALM 33:22

I wait for you, O LORD;
you will answer, O Lord my GOD.

PSALM 38:15

Lord, what do I look for?
My hope is in you.

PSALM 39:7

Why are you downcast, O my soul?
Why so disturbed within me?
Put your hope in God,
for I will yet praise him,
my Savior and my God.

PSALM 43:5

You have been my hope, O Sovereign LORD,
my confidence since my youth.

PSALM 71:5

As for me, I will always have hope;
>   I will praise God more and more.

PSALM 71:14

May those who fear God rejoice when they see me,
>   for I have put my hope in your word.

PSALM 119:74

Sustain me according to your
>   promise, and I will live;
>   do not let my hopes be dashed.

PSALM 119:116

Put your hope in the LORD,
>   for with the LORD is unfailing love
>   and with him is full redemption.

PSALM 130:7

Blessed is he whose help is the God of Jacob,
>   whose hope is in the LORD his God,
the Maker of heaven and earth,
>   the sea, and everything in them—
>   the LORD, who remains faithful forever.

PSALM 146:5–6

Hope deferred makes the heart sick,
>   but a longing fulfilled is a tree of life.

PROVERBS 13:12

Know also that wisdom is sweet to your soul;
>   if you find it, there is a future hope for you,
>   and your hope will not be cut off.

PROVERBS 24:14

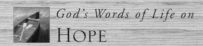
Blessed is the man who trusts in the LORD,
whose confidence is in him.
He will be like a tree planted by the water
that sends out its roots by the stream.
It does not fear when heat comes;
its leaves are always green.
It has no worries in a year of drought
and never fails to bear fruit.

JEREMIAH 17:7–8

Yet this I call to mind
Therefore I have hope:
Because of the LORD's great
love we are not consumed,
for his compassions never fail.

LAMENTATIONS 3:21–22

I say to myself, "The LORD is my portion;
therefore I will wait for him."
The LORD is good to those whose hope is in him,
to the one who seeks him.

LAMENTATIONS 3:24–25

In this hope we were saved. But hope that is seen
is no hope at all. Who hopes for what he already
has? But if we hope for what we do not yet have,
we wait for it patiently. ROMANS 8:24–25

Everything that was written in the past was written to teach us, so that through endurance and the encouragement of the Scriptures we might have hope.

ROMANS 15:4

May the God of hope fill you with all joy and peace as you trust in him, so that you may overflow with hope by the power of the Holy Spirit.

ROMANS 15:13

We continually remember before our God and Father your work produced by faith, your labor prompted by love, and your endurance inspired by hope in our Lord Jesus Christ.

1 THESSALONIANS 1:3

May our Lord Jesus Christ himself and God our Father, who loved us and by his grace gave us eternal encouragement and good hope, encourage your hearts and strengthen you in every good deed and word.

2 THESSALONIANS 2:16–17

We have God's hope as an anchor for the soul, firm and secure.

HEBREWS 6:19

We also rejoice in our sufferings, because we know that suffering produces perseverance; perseverance, character; and character, hope. And hope does not disappoint us, because God has poured out his love into our hearts by the Holy Spirit, whom he has given us.

ROMANS 5:3–5

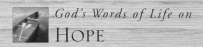
Faith is being sure of what we hope for and
certain of what we do not see.

HEBREWS 11:1

In your hearts set apart Christ as Lord. Always be
prepared to give an answer to everyone who asks
you to give the reason for the hope that you have.

1 PETER 3:15

Though he slay me, yet will I hope in him;
I will surely defend my ways to his face.

JOB 13:15

My heart is glad and my tongue rejoices;
my body also will live in hope,
because you will not abandon me to the grave,
nor will you let your Holy One see decay.
You have made known to me the paths of life;
you will fill me with joy in your presence.

ACTS 2:26–28

Be joyful in hope, . . . faithful in prayer.

ROMANS 12:12

All acts of hope expose themselves to ridicule because they seem impractical, failing to conform to visible reality. But in fact they are the reality that is being constructed but is not yet visible. Hope commits us to actions that connect with God's promises.

What we call hoping is often only wishing. We want things we think are impossible, but we have better sense than to spend any money or commit our lives to them.

Biblical hope, though, is an act. Hope acts on the conviction that God will complete the work that he has begun even when the appearances, especially when the appearances, oppose it.

Hope-determined actions participate in the future that God is bringing into being. These acts are rarely spectacular. Usually they take place outside sacred settings. Almost never are they perceived to be significant by bystanders.

It is not easy to act in hope because most of the immediate evidence is against it. It takes courage to act in hope. But it is the only practical action that survives the decay of the moment.

EUGENE H. PETERSON

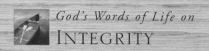
If anyone obeys his word, God's love is truly
made complete in him. This is how we know we
are in him.

1 JOHN 2:5

The LORD said to Satan, "Have you considered
my servant Job? There is no one on earth like
him; he is blameless and upright, a man who
fears God and shuns evil. And he still maintains
his integrity, though you incited me against him
to ruin him without any reason."

JOB 2:3

Job said, "I will never admit you are in the right;
till I die, I will not deny my integrity."

JOB 27:5

May integrity and uprightness protect me,
because my hope is in you.

PSALM 25:21

Righteousness guards the man of integrity,
but wickedness overthrows the sinner.

PROVERBS 13:6

I put in charge of Jerusalem my brother Hanani,
along with Hananiah the commander of the
citadel, because he was a man of integrity and
feared God more than most men do.

NEHEMIAH 7:2

He who walks righteously
        and speaks what is right,
who rejects gain from extortion
        and keeps his hand from accepting bribes,
who stops his ears against plots of murder
        and shuts his eyes against contemplating evil—
this is the man who will dwell on the heights,
        whose refuge will be the mountain fortress.
His bread will be supplied,
        and water will not fail him.

ISAIAH 33:15–16

Jesus said, "In everything, do to others what you would have them do to you, for this sums up the Law and the Prophets."

MATTHEW 7:12

I strive always to keep my conscience clear before God and man.

ACTS 24:16

We are taking pains to do what is right, not only in the eyes of the Lord but also in the eyes of men.

2 CORINTHIANS 8:21

Whatever is true, whatever is noble, whatever is right, whatever is pure, whatever is lovely, whatever is admirable—if anything is excellent or praiseworthy—think about such things.

PHILIPPIANS 4:8

Pray for us. We are sure that we have a clear conscience and desire to live honorably in every way.

HEBREWS 13:18

Slaves, obey your earthly masters in everything; and do it, not only when their eye is on you and to win their favor, but with sincerity of heart and reverence for the Lord. Whatever you do, work at it with all your heart, as working for the Lord, not for men.

COLOSSIANS 3:22–23

Make it your ambition to lead a quiet life, to mind your own business and to work with your hands, just as we told you, so that your daily life may win the respect of outsiders and so that you will not be dependent on anybody.

1 THESSALONIANS 4:11–12

Live such good lives among the pagans that, though they accuse you of doing wrong, they may see your good deeds and glorify God on the day he visits us.

1 PETER 2:12

Select capable men from all the people— men who fear God, trustworthy men who hate dishonest gain.

EXODUS 18:21

In everything set them an example by doing what is good. In your teaching show integrity, seriousness and soundness of speech that cannot be condemned, so that those who oppose you may be ashamed because they have nothing bad to say about us.

TITUS 2:7–8

Let the LORD judge the peoples.
Judge me, O LORD, according to my righteousness,
according to my integrity, O Most High.

PSALM 7:8

LORD, who may dwell in your sanctuary?
Who may live on your holy hill?
He whose walk is blameless
and who does what is righteous,
who speaks the truth from his heart.

PSALM 15:1–2

Do not pervert justice or show partiality. Do not accept a bribe, for a bribe blinds the eyes of the wise and twists the words of the righteous. Follow justice and justice alone, so that you may live and possess the land the LORD your God is giving you.

DEUTERONOMY 16:19–20

The man of integrity walks securely,
but he who takes crooked
paths will be found out.

PROVERBS 10:9

The integrity of the upright guides them,
but the unfaithful are
destroyed by their duplicity.
PROVERBS 11:3

He has showed you, O man, what is good.
And what does the LORD require of you?
To act justly and to love mercy
and to walk humbly with your God.
MICAH 6:8

Whoever can be trusted with very little can also
be trusted with much, and whoever is dishonest
with very little will also be dishonest with much.
LUKE 16:10

I know, my God, that you test the heart and are
pleased with integrity. All these things have I
given willingly and with honest intent.
1 CHRONICLES 29:17

A father has to be careful of his promises, because a real man will follow through.

A real man is a man of integrity. That means going all out in everything he does. When he says something, you can count on it, take it to the bank. If I say I'm going to do something, you can consider it done. The first time I violate that, my credibility is shot. Our reputations are only as good as our last performances.

Unless the real men of this country—and there aren't many left—come together and align themselves under God, we're headed for catastrophe. God is looking for men who will obey and be what he wants them to be.

MIKE SINGLETARY

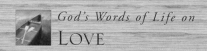
Do not seek revenge or bear a grudge against one of your people, but love your neighbor as yourself. I am the LORD.

LEVITICUS 19:18

Jesus said, "My command is this: Love each other as I have loved you. Greater love has no one than this, that he lay down his life for his friends."

JOHN 15:12–13

Be devoted to one another in brotherly love. Honor one another above yourselves.

ROMANS 12:10

You, my brothers, were called to be free. But do not use your freedom to indulge the sinful nature; rather, serve one another in love. The entire law is summed up in a single command: "Love your neighbor as yourself."

GALATIANS 5:13–14

How good and pleasant it is
when brothers live together
in unity!

PSALM 133:1

As we have opportunity, let us do good to all people, especially to those who belong to the family of believers.

GALATIANS 6:10

Live a life of love, just as Christ loved us and gave himself up for us as a fragrant offering and sacrifice to God.
EPHESIANS 5:2

May the Lord make your love increase and overflow for each other and for everyone else, just as ours does for you.
1 THESSALONIANS 3:12

About brotherly love we do not need to write to you, for you yourselves have been taught by God to love each other.
1 THESSALONIANS 4:9

Keep on loving each other as brothers.
HEBREWS 13:1

If you really keep the royal law found in Scripture, "Love your neighbor as yourself," you are doing right.
JAMES 2:8

Hatred stirs up dissension,
but love covers over all wrongs.
PROVERBS 10:12

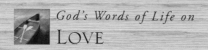

Live in harmony with one another; be sympathetic,
love as brothers, be compassionate and humble.
Do not repay evil with evil or insult with insult,
but with blessing, because to this you were called
so that you may inherit a blessing.

1 PETER 3:8–9

A new command I give you: Love one another.
As I have loved you, so you must love one
another. By this all men will know that you are
my disciples, if you love one another.

JOHN 13:34–35

Now that you have purified yourselves by obeying
the truth so that you have sincere love for your
brothers, love one another deeply, from the heart.

1 PETER 1:22

Dear friends, let us love one another, for love
comes from God. Everyone who loves has been
born of God and knows God. Whoever does not
love does not know God, because God is love.

1 JOHN 4:7–8

No one has ever seen God; but if we love one
another, God lives in us and his love is made
complete in us.

1 JOHN 4:12

Christ has given us this command: Whoever loves God must also love his brother.

1 JOHN 4:21

If I speak in the tongues of men and of angels, but have not love, I am only a resounding gong or a clanging cymbal. If I have the gift of prophecy and can fathom all mysteries and all knowledge, and if I have a faith that can move mountains, but have not love, I am nothing. If I give all I possess to the poor and surrender my body to the flames, but have not love, I gain nothing. Love is patient, love is kind. It does not envy, it does not boast, it is not proud. It is not rude, it is not self-seeking, it is not easily angered, it keeps no record of wrongs. Love does not delight in evil but rejoices with the truth. It always protects, always trusts, always hopes, always perseveres. Love never fails.

1 CORINTHIANS 13:1–8

In Christ Jesus neither circumcision nor uncircumcision has any value. The only thing that counts is faith expressing itself through love.

GALATIANS 5:6

The fruit of the Spirit is love, joy, peace, patience, kindness, goodness, faithfulness.

GALATIANS 5:22

God did not give us a spirit of timidity, but a spirit of power, of love and of self-discipline.

2 TIMOTHY 1:7

Jesus said, "God so loved the world that he gave his one and only Son, that whoever believes in him shall not perish but have eternal life."

JOHN 3:16

Above all, love each other deeply, because love covers over a multitude of sins.

1 PETER 4:8

These three remain: faith, hope and love. But the greatest of these is love.

1 CORINTHIANS 13:13

Jesus replied: "'Love the Lord your God with all your heart and with all your soul and with all your mind.' This is the first and greatest commandment. And the second is like it: 'Love your neighbor as yourself.' All the Law and the Prophets hang on these two commandments."

MATTHEW 22:37–38

When Jesus was asked to name the great commandments in the Scriptures, he didn't hesitate in the least. He told a young lawyer, "Love the Lord your God with all your heart and with all your soul and with all your mind. Love your neighbor as yourself" (Matthew 22:37, 39). Loving God, loving others and finding value in ourselves. Without a doubt, these three aspects of love are the most effective weapons against the destructive power of low self-worth.

Genuine love is a gift we give others. It isn't purchased by their actions or contingent upon our emotions at the moment. It may carry with it strong emotional feelings, but it isn't supported by them. Rather, it is a decision we make on a daily basis that someone is special and valuable to us. In fact, love for someone often begins to flow once we have made the decision to honor them.

GARY SMALLEY AND JOHN TRENT

He has showed you, O man,
what is good.
And what does the Lord
require of you?
To act justly and to love mercy
and to walk humbly with
your God.

MICAH 6:8

Jesus said, "Blessed are the merciful, for they will be shown mercy."

MATTHEW 5:7

Jesus said, "Be merciful, just as your Father is merciful."

LUKE 6:36

Judgment without mercy will be shown to anyone who has not been merciful. Mercy triumphs over judgment!

JAMES 2:13

The LORD said, " ... I will have mercy on whom I will have mercy, and I will have compassion on whom I will have compassion."

EXODUS 33:19

Praise be to the LORD,
for he has heard my cry for mercy.

PSALM 28:6

Let the wicked forsake his way
and the evil man his thoughts.
Let him turn to the LORD, and
he will have mercy on him,
and to our God, for he will freely pardon.

ISAIAH 55:7

Do not withhold your mercy from me, O LORD;
may your love and your truth always protect me.

PSALM 40:11

Answer me, O LORD, out of the
goodness of your love;
in your great mercy turn to me.

PSALM 69:16

In all their distress [God] too was distressed,
and the angel of his presence saved them.
In his love and mercy he redeemed them;
he lifted them up and carried them
all the days of old.

ISAIAH 63:9

O LORD, hear my prayer,
listen to my cry for mercy;
in your faithfulness and righteousness
come to my relief.

PSALM 143:1

I desire mercy, not sacrifice,
and acknowledgment of God
rather than burnt offerings.

HOSEA 6:6

Who is a God like you,
who pardons sin and forgives the transgression
of the remnant of his inheritance?
You do not stay angry forever
but delight to show mercy.

MICAH 7:18

This is what the LORD Almighty says:
"Administer true justice; show mercy and
compassion to one another." ZECHARIAH 7:9

He who conceals his sins does
not prosper,
but whoever confesses and
renounces them finds mercy.

PROVERBS 28:13

His mercy extends to those who fear him,
from generation to generation. LUKE 1:50

God says to Moses, "I will have mercy on whom I
have mercy, and I will have compassion on whom
I have compassion." It does not, therefore, depend
on man's desire or effort, but on God's mercy.

ROMANS 9:15–16

If it is encouraging, let him encourage; if it is
contributing to the needs of others, let him give
generously; if it is leadership, let him govern
diligently; if it is showing mercy, let him do
it cheerfully. ROMANS 12:8

I urge you, brothers, in view of God's mercy, to offer your bodies as living sacrifices, holy and pleasing to God—this is your spiritual act of worship.

ROMANS 12:1

Let us then approach the throne of grace with confidence, so that we may receive mercy and find grace to help us in our time of need.

HEBREWS 4:16

Because of his great love for us, God, who is rich in mercy, made us alive with Christ even when we were dead in transgressions—it is by grace you have been saved.

EPHESIANS 2:4–5

David said to Gad, "I am in deep distress. Let me fall into the hands of the LORD, for his mercy is very great; but do not let me fall into the hands of men."

1 CHRONICLES 21:13

At one time we too were foolish, disobedient, deceived and enslaved by all kinds of passions and pleasures. We lived in malice and envy, being hated and hating one another. But when the kindness and love of God our Savior appeared, he saved us, not because of righteous things we had done, but because of his mercy.

TITUS 3:3–5

The wisdom that comes from heaven is first of all
pure; then peace-loving, considerate, submissive,
full of mercy and good fruit, impartial and sincere.

JAMES 3:17

Mercy, peace and love be yours in abundance.

JUDE V. 2

I knew that you are a gracious and compassionate
God, slow to anger and abounding in love, a God
who relents from sending calamity.

JONAH 4:2

Nothing expresses God's yearning to forgive better than the Book of Jonah. It contains but one line of prophecy: "Forty more days and Nineveh will be overturned" (3:4). But, to Jonah's disgust, that simple announcement of doom sparked a spiritual revival in hated Nineveh and changed God's plans for punishment.

Jonah, sulking under a shriveled vine, admitted he had suspected God's soft heart all along. Thus the whole madcap scenario of balky prophet, ocean storm, and whale detour came about because Jonah could not trust God—could not, that is, trust him to be harsh and unrelenting toward Nineveh.

As Robert Frost summed up the story, "After Jonah, you could never trust God not to be merciful again."

PHILIP YANCEY

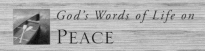

You will keep in perfect peace
him whose mind is steadfast,
because he trusts in you.
ISAIAH 26:3

Jesus himself is our peace, who has made the two one and has destroyed the barrier, the dividing wall of hostility.
EPHESIANS 2:14

LORD, *you establish peace for us;*
all that we have accomplished
you have done for us.
ISAIAH 26:12

Whatever you have learned or received or heard from me, or seen in me—put it into practice. And the God of peace will be with you.
PHILIPPIANS 4:9

Let the peace of Christ rule in your hearts, since as members of one body you were called to peace. And be thankful.
COLOSSIANS 3:15

Do not be anxious about anything, but in everything, by prayer and petition, with thanksgiving, present your requests to God. And the peace of God, which transcends all understanding, will guard your hearts and your minds in Christ Jesus.
PHILIPPIANS 4:6–7

There will be trouble and distress for every
human being who does evil...but glory, honor
and peace for everyone who does good.

ROMANS 2:9–10

I will lie down and sleep in peace,
for you alone, O LORD,
make me dwell in safety.

PSALM 4:8

Jesus said, "Peace I leave with you; my peace I
give you. I do not give to you as the world gives.
Do not let your hearts be troubled and do not
be afraid."

JOHN 14:27

The LORD gives strength to his people;
the LORD blesses his people with peace.

PSALM 29:11

Turn from evil and do good;
seek peace and pursue it.

PSALM 34:14

A heart at peace gives life to the body,
but envy rots the bones.

PROVERBS 14:30

The meek will inherit the land
and enjoy great peace.

PSALM 37:11

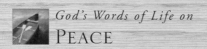
Great peace have they who love your law,
and nothing can make them stumble.

PSALM 119:165

The fruit of the Spirit is love, joy, peace, patience, kindness, goodness, faithfulness.

GALATIANS 5:22

Aim for perfection, listen to my appeal, be of one mind, live in peace. And the God of love and peace will be with you.

2 CORINTHIANS 13:11

Make every effort to keep the unity of the Spirit through the bond of peace.

EPHESIANS 4:3

If it is possible, as far as it depends on you, live at peace with everyone.

ROMANS 12:18

The wisdom that comes from heaven is first of all pure; then peace-loving, considerate, submissive, full of mercy and good fruit, impartial and sincere. Peacemakers who sow in peace raise a harvest of righteousness.

JAMES 3:17–18

When a man's ways are
pleasing to the LORD,
he makes even his enemies
live at peace with him.

PROVERBS 16:7

Let us therefore make very effort to do what leads to peace and to mutual edification.

ROMANS 14:19

Submit to God and be at peace with him;
in this way prosperity will come to you.

JOB 22:21

Consider the blameless, observe the upright;
there is a future for the man of peace.

PSALM 37:37

Discipline your son, and he will give you peace;
he will bring delight to your soul.

PROVERBS 29:17

The fruit of righteousness will be peace;
the effect of righteousness
will be quietness and confidence forever.

ISAIAH 32:17

Those who walk uprightly
enter into peace;
they find rest as they lie in death.

ISAIAH 57:2

"Do not be afraid, O man highly esteemed," he said. "Peace! Be strong now; be strong."

DANIEL 10:19

Jesus said, "Be at peace with each other."

MARK 9:50

Jesus said, "I have told you these things, so that in me you may have peace. In this world you will have trouble. But take heart! I have overcome the world."

JOHN 16:33

The mind of sinful man is death, but the mind controlled by the Spirit is life and peace.

ROMANS 8:6

I had a tiny taste of success and a tiny taste of religion—but not much Christianity. Sure, I was a good person. I treated others with respect.

But someone once described the contrast between a good life and a godly life as the difference between the top of the ocean and the bottom. On top, sometimes it's like glass—serene and calm—and other times it's raging and stormy. But hundreds of fathoms below, it is beautiful and consistent, always calm, always peaceful.

Down deep in my heart, I did not have the peace that comes only from knowing Jesus Christ as a personal Savior. Back then in 1970, when I was twenty-nine years old and a head football coach for the first time in my life, I was a church-goer and a professing Christian. But it wasn't until four years later, when I was a rookie assistant coach at the University of Michigan, that I discovered a real relationship with Jesus Christ. And when I accepted Christ as Savior and Lord of my life, I began an adventure that has transformed my life.

BILL MCCARTNEY

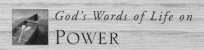
Jesus looked at them and said, "With man this is impossible, but with God all things are possible."
MATTHEW 19:26

I am the LORD, the God of all mankind. Is anything too hard for me?
JEREMIAH 32:27

The LORD is slow to anger and great in power;
the LORD will not leave the guilty unpunished.
His way is in the whirlwind and the storm,
and clouds are the dust of his feet.
NAHUM 1:3

See now that I myself am He!
There is no god besides me.
I put to death and I bring to life,
I have wounded and I will heal,
and no one can deliver out of my hand.
DEUTERONOMY 32:39

All the peoples of the earth
are regarded as nothing.
God does as he pleases
with the powers of heaven
and the peoples of the earth.
No one can hold back his hand
or say to him: "What have
you done?"
DANIEL 4:35

Wealth and honor come from you;
you are the ruler of all things.
In your hands are strength and power
to exalt and give strength to all.
Now, our God, we give you thanks,
and praise your glorious name.

1 CHRONICLES 29:12–13

You are awesome, O God, in your sanctuary;
the God of Israel gives power
and strength to his people.
Praise be to God!

PSALM 68:35

God said, "I have raised you up for this very
purpose, that I might show you my power and that
my name might be proclaimed in all the earth."

EXODUS 9:16

Being strengthened with all power according to
his glorious might so that you may have great
endurance and patience.

COLOSSIANS 1:11

To God belong wisdom and power;
counsel and understanding are his.

JOB 12:13

[God's] wisdom is profound, his power is vast.
Who has resisted him and come out unscathed?

JOB 9:4

Great is our Lord and mighty in power;
his understanding has no limit.

PSALM 147:5

A wise man has great power,
and a man of knowledge
increases strength.

PROVERBS 24:5

Be strong in the Lord and in his mighty power.

EPHESIANS 6:10

Yours, O LORD, is the greatness and the power
and the glory and the majesty and the splendor,
for everything in heaven and earth is yours.
Yours, O LORD, is the kingdom;
you are exalted as head over all.
Wealth and honor come from you;
you are the ruler of all things.
In your hands are strength and power
to exalt and give strength to all.

1 CHRONICLES 29:11–12

"This is the word of the LORD to Zerubbabel:
'Not by might nor by power, but by my Spirit,'
says the LORD Almighty."

ZECHARIAH 4:6

You may say to yourself, "My power and the
strength of my hands have produced this wealth
for me." But remember the LORD your God, for
it is he who gives you the ability to produce
wealth, and so confirms his covenant, which he
swore to your forefathers, as it is today.

DEUTERONOMY 8:17–18

What makes the temptation of power so seemingly irresistible?

Maybe it is that power offers an easy substitute for the hard task of love. It seems easier to be God than to love God, easier to control people than to love people, easier to own life than to love life.

The long painful history of the church is the history of people ever and again tempted to choose power over love, control over the cross, being a leader over being led.

Those who resisted this temptation to the end and thereby give us hope are the true saints.

HENRI NOUWEN

Before they call I will answer;
while they are still speaking
I will hear.

ISAIAH 65:24

Jesus said, "Whatever you ask for in prayer, believe that you have received it, and it will be yours."

MARK 11:24

Jesus said, "Ask and it will be given to you; seek and you will find; knock and the door will be opened to you. For everyone who asks receives; he who seeks finds; and to him who knocks, the door will be opened."

MATTHEW 7:7–8

Jesus said, "If you believe, you will receive whatever you ask for in prayer."

MATTHEW 21:22

Jesus said, "If two of you on earth agree about anything you ask for, it will be done for you by my Father in heaven. For where two or three come together in my name, there am I with them."

MATTHEW 18:19–20

Dear friends, if our hearts do not condemn us, we have confidence before God and receive from him anything we ask, because we obey his commands and do what pleases him.

1 JOHN 3:21–22

Jesus said, "When you pray, go into your room, close the door and pray to your Father, who is unseen. Then your Father, who sees what is done in secret, will reward you.

MATTHEW 6:6

The LORD is near to all who call on him,
*   to all who call on him in truth.*

PSALM 145:18

Jesus answered, "In that day you will no longer ask me anything. I tell you the truth, my Father will give you whatever you ask in my name. Until now you have not asked for anything in my name. Ask and you will receive, and your joy will be complete."

JOHN 16:23–24

Call to me and I will answer you and tell you great and unsearchable things you do not know.

JEREMIAH 33:3

"He will call upon me, and I
*   will answer him;*
*   I will be with him in trouble,*
*   I will deliver him and honor him,"*
*   says the LORD.*

PSALM 91:15

The LORD is far from the wicked
*   but he hears the prayer of the righteous.*

PROVERBS 15:29

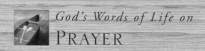
Delight yourself in the LORD
and he will give you the
desires of your heart.

PSALM 37:4

Jesus said, "If you remain in me and my words
remain in you, ask whatever you wish, and it will
be given you."

JOHN 15:7

Jesus said, "I will do whatever you ask in my
name, so that the Son may bring glory to the
Father. You may ask me for anything in my
name, and I will do it."

JOHN 14:13–14

I wait for you, O LORD;
you will answer, O Lord my God.

PSALM 38:15

If we confess our sins, God is faithful and just
and will forgive us our sins and purify us from
all unrighteousness.

1 JOHN 1:9

Very early in the morning, while it was still dark,
Jesus got up, left the house and went off to a
solitary place, where he prayed.

MARK 1:35

Jesus said, "When you pray, do not be like the hypocrites, for they love to pray standing in the synagogues and on the street corners to be seen by men. I tell you the truth, they have received their reward in full."

MATTHEW 6:5

Do not be anxious about anything, but in everything, by prayer and petition, with thanksgiving, present your requests to God. And the peace of God, which transcends all understanding, will guard your hearts and your minds in Christ Jesus.

PHILIPPIANS 4:6–7

Is any one of you in trouble? He should pray. Is anyone happy? Let him sing songs of praise. Is any one of you sick? He should call the elders of the church to pray over him and anoint him with oil in the name of the Lord. And the prayer offered in faith will make the sick person well; the Lord will raise him up. If he has sinned, he will be forgiven. Therefore confess your sins to each other and pray for each other so that you may be healed. The prayer of a righteous man is powerful and effective.

JAMES 5:13–16

This is the confidence we have in approaching God: that if we ask anything according to his will, he hears us. And if we know that he hears us—whatever we ask—we know that we have what we asked of him.

1 JOHN 5:14–15

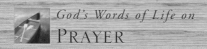
The eyes of the Lord are on the righteous
and his ears are attentive to their prayer.
1 PETER 3:12

Let us then approach the throne of grace with confidence, so that we may receive mercy and find grace to help us in our time of need.
HEBREWS 4:16

God said, "If my people, who are called by my name, will humble themselves and pray and seek my face and turn from their wicked ways, then will I hear from heaven and will forgive their sin and will heal their land."
2 CHRONICLES 7:14

Out of the depths I cry to you, O LORD;
O Lord, hear my voice.
Let your ears be attentive
to my cry for mercy
PSALM 130:1–2

The biblical Christian can only pray empty-handed, as the thirteenth-century Dominican preacher William Peraldus expressed it. Our hope depends not on the right technique or the proper phrase or gesture, which borders on magic, but on the promises of God.

As I see it, true prayer is neither mystical rapture nor ritual observance nor philosophical reflection: it is the outpouring of the soul before a living God, the crying to God "out of the depths." Such prayer can only be uttered by one convicted of sin by the grace of God and moved to confession by the Spirit of God.

True prayer is an encounter with the Holy in which we realize not only our creatureliness and guilt but also the joy of knowing that our sins are forgiven through the atoning death of the divine Savior, Jesus Christ. In such an encounter, we are impelled not only to bow before God and seek his mercy but also to offer thanksgiving for grace that goes out to undeserving sinners.

DONALD BLOESCH

To fear the LORD is to hate evil;
I hate pride and arrogance,
evil behavior and perverse speech.

PROVERBS 8:13

Pride only breeds quarrels,
but wisdom is found in
those who take advice.

PROVERBS 13:10

When pride comes, then comes disgrace,
but with humility comes wisdom.

PROVERBS 11:2

A man's pride brings him low,
but a man of lowly spirit gains honor.

PROVERBS 29:23

Jesus said, "Everyone who exalts himself will be
humbled, and he who humbles himself will
be exalted."

LUKE 18:14

By the grace given me I say to every one of you:
Do not think of yourself more highly than you
ought, but rather think of yourself with sober
judgment, in accordance with the measure of
faith God has given you.

ROMANS 12:3

The eyes of the arrogant man will be humbled
and the pride of men brought low;
the LORD alone will be exalted in that day.

ISAIAH 2:11

When some people begin to experience a degree of success, they become overly confident of their own abilities. They behave as if no one else in the world can do what they do. They get an exaggerated sense of their own importance and are puffed up with pride, making it difficult for most people to work with them.

These swollen-headed types also usually cease learning. Why shouldn't they? Don't they already know everything in their field (or assume they do)? Despite their talent, they lose their usefulness. Instead of singing the hymn "How Great Thou Art," their words sound like "How Great I Am." I have worked out a simple formula for humility.

IF WE RECOGNIZE THAT:
- God created this universe, including us, and
- God shows that he is much more powerful than we are by what he does and has done in our world, and
- God gives each of us abilities that we cannot supply to ourselves or explain our worthiness of,

THEN WE ARE HUMBLED.

BEN CARSON

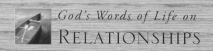

Bear with each other and forgive whatever
grievances you may have against one another.
Forgive as the Lord forgave you.

COLOSSIANS 3:13

Be completely humble and gentle; be patient,
bearing with one another in love. Make every
effort to keep the unity of the Spirit through
the bond of peace.

EPHESIANS 4:2–3

Do not be yoked together with unbelievers.
For what do righteousness and wickedness have
in common? Or what fellowship can light have
with darkness?...What does a believer have in
common with an unbeliever?...For we are the
temple of the living God. As God has said:
"I will live with them and walk among them,
and I will be their God, and they will be my
people." "Therefore come out from them and
be separate, says the Lord."

2 CORINTHIANS 6:14–17

By the grace given me I say to every one of you:
Do not think of yourself more highly than you
ought, but rather think of yourself with sober
judgment, in accordance with the measure of faith
God has given you. Just as each of us has one
body with many members, and these members do
not all have the same function, so in Christ we
who are many form one body, and each member
belongs to all the others.

ROMANS 12:3–5

Two are better than one,
    because they have a good
        return for their work:
If one falls down,
    his friend can help him up.
But pity the man who falls
    and has no one to help him up!
Though one may be overpowered,
    two can defend themselves.
A cord of three strands is not
        quickly broken.

ECCLESIASTES 4:9–10, 12

In everything set them an example by doing what is good. In your teaching show integrity, seriousness and soundness of speech that cannot be condemned, so that those who oppose you may be ashamed because they have nothing bad to say about us.

TITUS 2:7–8

As iron sharpens iron,
    so one man sharpens another.

PROVERBS 27:17

Peter began to speak: "I now realize how true it is that God does not show favoritism but accepts men from every nation who fear him and do what is right."

ACTS 10:34–35

The LORD does not look at the things man looks at. Man looks at the outward appearance, but the LORD looks at the heart.

1 SAMUEL 16:7

My brothers, as believers in our glorious Lord Jesus Christ, don't show favoritism.

JAMES 2:1

Jesus said, "See that you do not look down on one of these little ones. For I tell you that their angels in heaven always see the face of my Father in heaven."

MATTHEW 18:10

Do not rebuke an older man harshly, but exhort him as if he were your father. Treat younger men as brothers, older women as mothers, and younger women as sisters, with absolute purity.

1 TIMOTHY 5:1–2

Carry each other's burdens, and in this way you will fulfill the law of Christ.

GALATIANS 6:2

Give everyone what you owe him: If you owe taxes, pay taxes; if revenue, then revenue; if respect, then respect; if honor, then honor. Let no debt remain outstanding, except the continuing debt to love one another.

ROMANS 13:7–8

Peacemakers who sow in peace raise a harvest
of righteousness.

JAMES 3:18

Clothe yourselves with humility toward one
another, because, "God opposes the proud but
gives grace to the humble." Humble yourselves,
therefore, under God's mighty hand, that he may
lift you up.

1 PETER 5:5–6

Jesus said, "Whoever wants to become great
among you must be your servant, and whoever
wants to be first must be your slave—just as the
Son of Man did not come to be served, but to
serve, and to give his life as a ransom for many."

MATTHEW 20:26–28

The Lord's servant must not quarrel; instead,
he must be kind to everyone, able to teach, not
resentful. Those who oppose him he must gently
instruct, in the hope that God will grant them
repentance leading them to a knowledge of
the truth.

2 TIMOTHY 2:24–25

Love one another deeply, from the heart.

1 PETER 1:22

A man's wisdom gives him patience;
it is to his glory to overlook an offense.

PROVERBS 19:11

Jesus said, "Why do you look at the speck of sawdust in your brother's eye and pay no attention to the plank in your own eye? How can you say to your brother, 'Brother, let me take the speck out of your eye,' when you yourself fail to see the plank in your own eye? You hypocrite, first take the plank out of your eye, and then you will see clearly to remove the speck from your brother's eye."

LUKE 6:41–42

Let the peace of Christ rule in your hearts, since as members of one body you were called to peace. And be thankful. Let the word of Christ dwell in you richly as you teach and admonish one another with all wisdom, and as you sing psalms, hymns and spiritual songs with gratitude in your hearts to God. And whatever you do, whether in word or deed, do it all in the name of the Lord Jesus, giving thanks to God the Father through him.

COLOSSIANS 3:15–17

I appeal to you, brothers, in the name of our Lord Jesus Christ, that all of you agree with one another so that there may be no divisions among you and that you may be perfectly united in mind and thought.

1 CORINTHIANS 1:10

You get what you give out. You want a loving God? Then be loving. You want a merciful God? Then be merciful. Want God to forgive you? Then forgive your fellowman. Want God to condemn you? Then be an accusatory person. Want to put yourself above the rest of the world? Then get ready for a God who is going to strain out every judgmental thought you've ever had and measure all the thoughts and intents of your hidden heart by the same standard.

You and I as Christians need to realize that however acceptable our lives may be for the general audience, we still possess an R-rated heart, and we're as good as dead if we want God to meet us on any other ground than his grace and forgiveness.

The joy of this truth is that once I can believe that forgiveness for myself, then I can believe it for anybody. I have new eyes to see beyond my neighbor's sin and love him or her with the love of Christ.

JOHN FISCHER

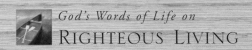
Love the LORD your God with all your heart and
with all your soul and with all your strength.

DEUTERONOMY 6:5

Be very careful to keep the commandment and
the law that Moses the servant of the LORD gave
you: to love the LORD your God, to walk in all
his ways, to obey his commands, to hold fast to
him and to serve him with all your heart and all
your soul.

JOSHUA 22:5

Since, then, you have been raised with Christ, set
your hearts on things above, where Christ is
seated at the right hand of God. Set your minds
on things above, not on earthly things.

COLOSSIANS 3:1–2

Blessed is the man
      who does not walk in the
            counsel of the wicked
or stand in the way of sinners
      or sit in the seat of mockers.
But his delight is in the law of the LORD,
      and on his law he meditates
            day and night.

PSALM 1:1–2

You desire truth in the inner parts;
      you teach me wisdom in the inmost place.

PSALM 51:6

You will keep in perfect peace
      him whose mind is steadfast,
      because he trusts in you.

ISAIAH 26:3

The mind of sinful man is death, but the mind controlled by the Spirit is life and peace.

ROMANS 8:6

The kingdom of God is not a matter of eating and drinking, but of righteousness, peace and joy in the Holy Spirit.

ROMANS 14:17

Jesus said, "Blessed are those who hunger and thirst for righteousness, for they will be filled."

MATTHEW 5:6

Jesus said, "Do not work for food that spoils, but for food that endures to eternal life, which the Son of Man will give you. On him God the Father has placed his seal of approval."

JOHN 6:27

Be careful that you do not forget the LORD your God, failing to observe his commands, his laws and his decrees that I am giving you this day. Otherwise, when you eat and are satisfied, when you build fine houses and settle down, and when your herds and flocks grow large and your silver and gold increase and all you have is multiplied, then your heart will become proud and you will forget the LORD your God.

DEUTERONOMY 8:11–14

Be careful, and watch yourselves closely so that you do not forget the things your eyes have seen or let them slip from your heart as long as you live. Teach them to your children and to their children after them.

DEUTERONOMY 4:9

This is what the LORD says:
"Stand at the crossroads and look;
ask for the ancient paths,
ask where the good way is, and walk in it,
and you will find rest for your souls."

JEREMIAH 6:16

Do your best to present yourself to God as one approved, a workman who does not need to be ashamed and who correctly handles the word of truth.

2 TIMOTHY 2:15

Being confident of this, that he who began a good work in you will carry it on to completion until the day of Christ Jesus.

PHILIPPIANS 1:6

This is my prayer: that your love may abound more and more in knowledge and depth of insight, so that you may be able to discern what is best and may be pure and blameless until the day of Christ.

PHILIPPIANS 1:9–10

Very few believers choose to drift; seldom do Christians plan to be lukewarm. But poor performance undermines confidence, and failure causes discouragement. Temptation, even when overcome, leaves us battle-scarred and weary. It is sometimes difficult to tell the difference between victory and defeat because issues are never clear-cut and our successes never total. When one has struggled through the testing time and finally endured, it seldom feels like triumph.

Someone has to help us at the time of our struggle. We need a brother in the hour of trial, and especially when we fail. Otherwise we fall into the discouragement of trying harder or of never quite measuring up. The subtle shift from trust in Christ to our own self-efforts robs us of hope and joy. We begin to tally hurts, count disappointments and weigh sacrifices. And already the drift has set in. We need the warning, but more than that, we need to know that we are known, understood and loved by someone who has marked out the path, has won the victory and is with us on the way. That someone is Jesus.

REUBEN R. WELCH

My son, keep my words
        and store up my commands within you.
Keep my commands and you will live;
        guard my teachings as the apple of your eye.
Bind them on your fingers;
        write them on the tablet of your heart.
                                PROVERBS 7:1-3

Jesus said, "As for the person who hears my words but does not keep them, I do not judge him. For I did not come to judge the world, but to save it. There is a judge for the one who rejects me and does not accept my words; that very word which I spoke will condemn him at the last day."
                                JOHN 12:47-48

I wish that all men were as I am. But each man has his own gift from God.
                                1 CORINTHIANS 7:7

When the kindness and love of God our Savior appeared, he saved us, not because of righteous things we had done, but because of his mercy. He saved us through the washing of rebirth and renewal by the Holy Spirit, whom he poured out on us generously through Jesus Christ our Savior, so that, having been justified by his grace, we might become heirs having the hope of eternal life. This is a trustworthy saying. And I want you to stress these things, so that those who have trusted in God may be careful to devote themselves to doing what is good. These things are excellent and profitable for everyone.
                                TITUS 3:4-8

Listen, my sons, to a father's instruction;
pay attention and gain understanding.

PROVERBS 4:1

To this you were called, because Christ suffered for you, leaving you an example, that you should follow in his steps.

1 PETER 2:21

Be imitators of God, therefore, as dearly loved children and live a life of love, just as Christ loved us and gave himself up for us as a fragrant offering and sacrifice to God.

EPHESIANS 5:1–2

Jesus said, "Whoever wants to become great among you must be your servant, and whoever wants to be first must be slave of all."

MARK 10:43–44

Jesus said, "I have set you an example that you should do as I have done for you."

JOHN 13:15

This is how we know what love is: Jesus Christ laid down his life for us. And we ought to lay down our lives for our brothers.

1 JOHN 3:16

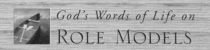
Dear children, let us not love with words or tongue but with actions and in truth.

1 JOHN 3:18

Don't let anyone look down on you because you are young, but set an example for the believers in speech, in life, in love, in faith and in purity.

1 TIMOTHY 4:12

In everything set them an example by doing what is good. In your teaching show integrity, seriousness and soundness of speech that cannot be condemned, so that those who oppose you may be ashamed because they have nothing bad to say about us.

TITUS 2:7–8

Be shepherds of God's flock that is under your care, serving as overseers—not because you must, but because you are willing, as God wants you to be; not greedy for money, but eager to serve; not lording it over those entrusted to you, but being examples to the flock.

1 PETER 5:2–3

God will turn the hearts of the fathers to their children, and the hearts of the children to their fathers.

MALACHI 4:6

Little boys are the hope of the next generation. They are the fathers of tomorrow. They must know who they are and what they are to do. They must see their role model in action. That's how they will know what it means to be a male. That puts the ball in my court … and in yours.

It's our job to save the boys. So the question is, how are we going to do that? I must have a pretty clear idea of what I need to teach them. I must ask myself: What do I specifically need to do in order to train them to become leaders of their families?

It is my job … to model for them the importance of …

knowing and obeying Jesus Christ,
knowing and displaying godly character,
knowing and loving my wife,
knowing and loving my children, and
knowing my gifts and abilities.

Then I can work hard and effectively in an area of strength, rather than weakness, and contribute effectively to the lives of others—and have a little fun at the same time.

STEVE FARRAR

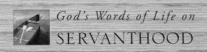
Jesus said, "Whoever wants to become great among you must be your servant, and whoever wants to be first must be slave of all."

MARK 10:43–44

Jesus said, "The greatest among you should be like the youngest, and the one who rules like the one who serves. For who is greater, the one who is at the table or the one who serves? Is it not the one who is at the table? But I am among you as one who serves."

LUKE 22:26–27

Jesus said, "I have set you an example that you should do as I have done for you. I tell you the truth, no servant is greater than his master, nor is a messenger greater than the one who sent him."

JOHN 13:15–16

Though I am free and belong to no man, I make myself a slave to everyone, to win as many as possible. To the Jews I became like a Jew, to win the Jews. To those under the law I became like one under the law (though I myself am not under the law), so as to win those under the law. To those not having the law I became like one not having the law (though I am not free from God's law but am under Christ's law), so as to win those not having the law. To the weak I became weak, to win the weak. I have become all things to all men so that by all possible means I might save some.

1 CORINTHIANS 9:19–22

Jesus said, "The greatest among you will be your servant."

MATTHEW 23:11

Your attitude should be the same as that of Christ Jesus: Who, being in very nature God, did not consider equality with God something to be grasped, but made himself nothing, taking the very nature of a servant, being made in human likeness. And being found in appearance as a man, he humbled himself and became obedient to death—even death on a cross!

PHILIPPIANS 2:5–8

Be very careful to keep the commandment and the law that Moses the servant of the LORD gave you: to love the LORD your God, to walk in all his ways, to obey his commands, to hold fast to him and to serve him with all your heart and all your soul.

JOSHUA 22:5

There are different kinds of service, but the same Lord.

1 CORINTHIANS 12:5

Jesus said, "Whoever wants to save his life will lose it, but whoever loses his life for me will find it."

MATTHEW 16:25

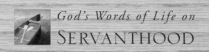
It is the LORD your God you must follow, and him you must revere. Keep his commands and obey him; serve him and hold fast to him.

DEUTERONOMY 13:4

Worship the Lord your God, and serve him only.

MATTHEW 4:10

If serving the LORD seems undesirable to you, then choose for yourselves this day whom you will serve, whether the gods your forefathers served beyond the River, or the gods of the Amorites, in whose land you are living. But as for me and my household, we will serve the LORD.

JOSHUA 24:15

Be devoted to one another in brotherly love. Honor one another above yourselves. Never be lacking in zeal, but keep your spiritual fervor, serving the Lord.

ROMANS 12:10–11

O Israel, what does the LORD your God ask of you but to fear the LORD your God, to walk in all his ways, to love him, to serve the LORD your God with all your heart and with all your soul, and to observe the LORD's commands and decrees that I am giving you today for your own good?

DEUTERONOMY 10:12–13

Be sure to fear the LORD and serve him faithfully with all your heart; consider what great things he has done for you.

1 SAMUEL 12:24

Jesus said, "Whoever wants to become great among you must be your servant, and whoever wants to be first must be your slave."

MATTHEW 20:26–27

Jesus said to them, "Whoever welcomes this little child in my name welcomes me; and whoever welcomes me welcomes the one who sent me. For he who is least among you all—he is the greatest."

LUKE 9:48

If anyone speaks, he should do it as one speaking the very words of God. If anyone serves, he should do it with the strength God provides, so that in all things God may be praised through Jesus Christ. To him be the glory and the power for ever and ever. Amen.

1 PETER 4:11

You, my brothers, were called to be free. But do not use your freedom to indulge the sinful nature; rather, serve one another in love.

GALATIANS 5:13

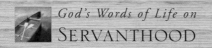
Sitting down, Jesus called the Twelve and said, "If anyone wants to be first, he must be the very last, and the servant of all."

MARK 9:35

Jesus said, "The man who loves his life will lose it, while the man who hates his life in this world will keep it for eternal life. Whoever serves me must follow me; and where I am, my servant also will be. My Father will honor the one who serves me."

JOHN 12:25–26

Jesus said, "My command is this: Love each other as I have loved you. Greater love has no one than this, that he lay down his life for his friends. You are my friends if you do what I command. I no longer call you servants, because a servant does not know his master's business. Instead, I have called you friends, for everything that I learned from my Father I have made known to you. You did not choose me, but I chose you and appointed you to go and bear fruit—fruit that will last. Then the Father will give you whatever you ask in my name. This is my command: Love each other."

JOHN 15:12–17

Leadership shared in mutual respect can establish a climate of dignity, freedom and responsibility, creating an atmosphere which is both comforting and stimulating … a Christian atmosphere.

But where one seizes power, or struggles for control, an atmosphere of competition and conflict chokes communication and understanding.

Leadership is a function which should always be shared. Authority in one area or another is a responsibility which is mutually designated to one or the other through honest negotiation. It can be renegotiated at any time.

To be a man—is to possess the strength to love another, not the need to dominate over others.

To be a man—is to experience the courage to accept another, not the compulsion to be an aggressor.

To be a man—is to keep faith with human values in relationships, not to value oneself by position or possessions.

To be a man—is to be free to give love and to be free to accept love in return.

DAVID AUGSBURGER

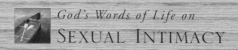
Let your eyes look straight ahead,
    fix your gaze directly before you.
Make level paths for your feet
    and take only ways that are firm.
Do not swerve to the right or the left;
    keep your foot from evil.

PROVERBS 4:25–27

It is God's will that you should be sanctified: that you should avoid sexual immorality; that each of you should learn to control his own body in a way that is holy and honorable, not in passionate lust like the heathen, who do not know God. For God did not call us to be impure, but to live a holy life.

1 THESSALONIANS 4:3–5, 7

Flee from sexual immorality. All other sins a man commits are outside his body, but he who sins sexually sins against his own body. Do you not know that your body is a temple of the Holy Spirit, who is in you, whom you have received from God? You are not your own; you were bought at a price. Therefore honor God with your body.

1 CORINTHIANS 6:18–20

Everything in the world—the cravings of sinful man, the lust of his eyes and the boasting of what he has and does—comes not from the Father but from the world. The world and its desires pass away, but the man who does the will of God lives forever.

1 JOHN 2:16–17

Turn my eyes away from worthless things;
preserve my life according to your word.

PSALM 119:37

Each one is tempted when, by his own evil desire, he is dragged away and enticed. Then, after desire has conceived, it gives birth to sin; and sin, when it is full-grown, gives birth to death. Don't be deceived, my dear brothers.

JAMES 1:14–16

A man's ways are in full view of the LORD,
and he examines all his paths.

PROVERBS 5:21

Husbands ought to love their wives as their own bodies. He who loves his wife loves himself. After all, no one ever hated his own body, but he feeds and cares for it, just as Christ does the church.

EPHESIANS 5:28–29

No temptation has seized you except what is common to man. And God is faithful; he will not let you be tempted beyond what you can bear. But when you are tempted, he will also provide a way out so that you can stand up under it.

1 CORINTHIANS 10:13

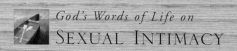

Among you there must not be even a hint of sexual immorality, or of any kind of impurity, or of greed, because these are improper for God's holy people.

EPHESIANS 5:3

Since there is so much immorality, each man should have his own wife, and each woman her own husband. The husband should fulfill his marital duty to his wife, and likewise the wife to her husband. The wife's body does not belong to her alone but also to her husband. In the same way, the husband's body does not belong to him alone but also to his wife. Do not deprive each other except by mutual consent and for a time, so that you may devote yourselves to prayer. Then come together again so that Satan will not tempt you because of your lack of self-control.

1 CORINTHIANS 7:2–5

I made a covenant with my eyes
not to look lustfully at a girl.

JOB 31:1

A one-woman kind of man is a man who demonstrates his commitment by disciplining his eyes. We are all familiar with the guy who can't walk one block without giving some woman the once-over from head to toe. He will even stop dead in his tracks in the flow of pedestrian traffic to turn and watch her as she goes by. Most of us are a little better socially adjusted than that.

A man who is committed with his eyes will avoid certain kinds of magazines and television programs. A hotel room on the road can be a very dangerous place for a one-woman kind of man who is not prepared for battle. When I bought a newspaper this morning, it was surrounded by pornographic magazines with alluring covers. "Girls of the Southwest Conference!" blazed the cover. If I don't discipline my eyes and look away, I'm going to start wondering how those girls in the Southwest Conference are getting along. And I must particularly cultivate that blindness away from home. I know I must do this because I know myself. And the self I know has a hard enough time even when I'm not away from home.

STEVE FARRAR

The LORD gives strength to his people;
the LORD blesses his people with peace.

PSALM 29:11

Do not fear, for I am with you;
do not be dismayed, for I am your God.
I will strengthen you and help you;
I will uphold you with my righteous right hand.

ISAIAH 41:10

God said to me, "My grace is sufficient for you, for my power is made perfect in weakness." Therefore I will boast all the more gladly about my weaknesses, so that Christ's power may rest on me. That is why, for Christ's sake, I delight in weaknesses, in insults, in hardships, in persecutions, in difficulties. For when I am weak, then I am strong.

2 CORINTHIANS 12:9–10

I can do everything through Christ who gives me strength.

PHILIPPIANS 4:13

Being strengthened with all power according to his glorious might so that you may have great endurance and patience, and joyfully giving thanks to the Father, who has qualified you to share in the inheritance of the saints in the kingdom of light.

COLOSSIANS 1:11–12

The LORD is the strength of his people,
a fortress of salvation for his anointed one.

PSALM 28:8

They will say of me "In the LORD alone
are righteousness and strength."

ISAIAH 45:24

Be strong in the Lord and in his mighty power.

EPHESIANS 6:10

I pray that out of his glorious riches he may
strengthen you with power through his Spirit in
your inner being, so that Christ may dwell in
your hearts through faith.

EPHESIANS 3:16–17

You are awesome, O God, in your sanctuary;
the God of Israel gives power
and strength to his people.
Praise be to God!

PSALM 68:35

Those who hope in the LORD
will renew their strength.
They will soar on wings like eagles;
they will run and not grow weary,
they will walk and not be faint.

ISAIAH 40:31

"I will strengthen them in the LORD
and in his name they will walk,"
declares the LORD.

ZECHARIAH 10:12

Wealth and honor come from you;
*   you are the ruler of all things.*
In your hands are strength and power
*   to exalt and give strength to all.*

1 CHRONICLES 29:12

The righteous will hold to their ways,
*   and those with clean hands*
*   will grow stronger.*

JOB 17:9

We do not lose heart. Though outwardly we are
wasting away, yet inwardly we are being renewed
day by day.

2 CORINTHIANS 4:16

Since we are surrounded by such a great cloud of
witnesses, let us throw off everything that hinders
and the sin that so easily entangles, and let us run
with perseverance the race marked out for us.

HEBREWS 12:1

My soul is weary with sorrow;
*   strengthen me according to your word.*

PSALM 119:28

The LORD gives strength to the weary
*   and increases the power of the weak.*

ISAIAH 40:29

Whenever there is the experience of weariness or degradation, you may be certain you have done one of two things— either you have disregarded a law of nature, or you have deliberately got out of touch with God.

There is no such thing as weariness in God's work. If you are in tune with the joy of God, the more you spend out in God's service, the more the recuperation goes on, and when once the warning note of weariness is given, it is a sign that something has gone wrong. If only we would heed the warning, we would find it is God's wonderfully gentle way of saying—"Not that way; that must be left alone; this must be given up."

Spiritual fatigue comes from the unconscious frittering away of God's time. When you feel weary or are exhausted, don't ask for hot milk, but get back to God. The secret of weariness and nervous disease in the natural world is a lack of a dominating interest, and the same is true in spiritual life. It is Christian activity that counts … and every moment is filled with an energy that is not our own, a super-abounding life that nothing can stand before.

OSWALD CHAMBERS

Jesus said, "Come to me, all you who are weary and burdened, and I will give you rest. Take my yoke upon you and learn from me, for I am gentle and humble in heart, and you will find rest for your souls. For my yoke is easy and my burden is light."

MATTHEW 11:28–30

Be strong in the Lord and in his mighty power.

EPHESIANS 6:10

The LORD gives strength to the weary
and increases the power of the weak.
Even youths grow tired and weary,
and young men stumble and fall;
but those who hope in the LORD
will renew their strength.
They will soar on wings like eagles;
they will run and not grow weary,
they will walk and not be faint.

ISAIAH 40:29–31

Remember the Sabbath day by keeping it holy. Six days you shall labor and do all your work, but the seventh day is a Sabbath to the LORD your God. On it you shall not do any work, neither you, nor your son or daughter, nor your manservant or maidservant, nor your animals, nor the alien within your gates. For in six days the LORD made the heavens and the earth, the sea, and all that is in them, but he rested on the seventh day. Therefore the LORD blessed the Sabbath day and made it holy.

EXODUS 20:8–11

This is what the Sovereign Lord,
the Holy One of Israel, says:

"In repentance and rest is your salvation,
in quietness and trust is your strength,
but you would have none of it."

ISAIAH 30:15

Do not fear, for I am with you;
do not be dismayed, for I am your God.
I will strengthen you and help you;
I will uphold you with my
righteous right hand.

ISAIAH 41:10

"I will refresh the weary and satisfy the faint,"
says the LORD.

JEREMIAH 31:25

Unless the LORD builds the house,
its builders labor in vain.
Unless the LORD watches over the city,
the watchmen stand guard in vain.
In vain you rise early
and stay up late,
toiling for food to eat—
for he grants sleep to those he loves.

PSALM 127:1–2

Let us not become weary in doing good, for at
the proper time we will reap a harvest if we do
not give up.

GALATIANS 6:9

He makes me lie down in green pastures,
he leads me beside quiet waters,
  he restores my soul.
He guides me in paths of righteousness
  for his name's sake.

PSALM 23:2–3

Since the promise of entering his rest still stands,
let us be careful that none of you be found to
have fallen short of it.

HEBREWS 4:1

By the seventh day God had finished the work he
had been doing; so on the seventh day he rested
from all his work.

GENESIS 2:2

There remains, then, a Sabbath-rest for the
people of God; for anyone who enters God's rest
also rests from his own work, just as God did
from his. Let us, therefore, make every effort to
enter that rest, so that no one will fall by
following their example of disobedience.

HEBREWS 4:9–11

Because so many people were coming and going
that they did not even have a chance to eat, Jesus
said to them, "Come with me by yourselves to a
quiet place and get some rest."

MARK 6:31

T oo much stress—especially stress that is not relieved by times of rest and renewal— can harm us physically, mentally and spiritually.

To a great extent Christians are caught up in the same rat race as everyone else. We have let our values become distorted and don't see life clearly from God's perspective. We've lost some of our distinctiveness; our lives are almost identical to those of people who are not committed to Christ. As a result, I believe we are violating very basic laws that God has set down for our bodies. And we may be doing all this in the name of the One who came to save us from our need to earn salvation!

Christians must wake up to the fact that they are burning themselves out just as quickly as everyone else is! Change is occurring so rapidly and hurry sickness is so rampant in our society that avoiding stress damage takes an extra effort. And the sad fact is that relatively few people—even Christians—are making that extra effort.

ARCHIBALD HART

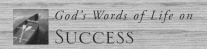

Be strong and very courageous. Be careful to obey all the law my servant Moses gave you; do not turn from it to the right or to the left, that you may be successful wherever you go. Do not let this Book of the Law depart from your mouth; meditate on it day and night, so that you may be careful to do everything written in it. Then you will be prosperous and successful.

JOSHUA 1:7–8

You will have success if you are careful to observe the decrees and laws that the LORD gave Moses for Israel. Be strong and courageous. Do not be afraid or discouraged.

1 CHRONICLES 22:13

King Uzziah sought God during the days of Zechariah, who instructed him in the fear of God. As long as he sought the LORD, God gave him success.

2 CHRONICLES 26:5

Blessed is the man
      who does not walk in the counsel of the wicked
or stand in the way of sinners
      or sit in the seat of mockers.
But his delight is in the law of the LORD,
      and on his law he meditates day and night.
He is like a tree planted by streams of water,
      which yields its fruit in season
and whose leaf does not wither.
      Whatever he does prospers.

PSALM 1:1–3

When his master saw that the LORD was with him and that the LORD gave him success in everything he did, Joseph found favor in his eyes and became his attendant. Potiphar put him in charge of his household, and he entrusted to his care everything he owned.

GENESIS 39:3–4

"I am about to go the way of all the earth," David said. "So be strong, show yourself a man, and observe what the LORD your God requires: Walk in his ways, and keep his decrees and commands, his laws and requirements, . . . so that you may prosper in all you do and wherever you go."

1 KINGS 2:2–3

In everything that Hezekiah undertook in the service of God's temple and in obedience to the law and the commands, he sought his God and worked wholeheartedly. And so he prospered.

2 CHRONICLES 31:21

May he give you the desire of your heart
 and make all your plans succeed.
We will shout for joy when you are victorious
 and will lift up our banners
 in the name of our God.
May the LORD grant all your requests.

PSALM 20:4–5

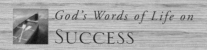
Have faith in the LORD your God and you will be upheld; have faith in his prophets and you will be successful.

2 CHRONICLES 20:20

Be on your guard; stand firm in the faith; be men of courage; be strong.

1 CORINTHIANS 16:13

May these words of mine, which I have prayed before the LORD, be near to the LORD our God day and night, that he may uphold the cause of his servant and the cause of his people Israel according to each day's need, so that all the peoples of the earth may know that the LORD is God and that there is no other.

1 KINGS 8:59–60

With everything imaginable working in his favor, it seemed Solomon would gratefully follow God. His prayer of dedication for the temple in 1 Kings 8 is one of the most majestic ever prayed.

Yet by the end of his reign Solomon had squandered away nearly every advantage. Along the way he lost sight of the original vision to which God had called him. Success in the kingdom of this world had crowded out interest in the kingdom of God. The brief, shining vision of a covenant nation faded away, and God withdrew his sanction. Solomon got whatever he wanted, especially when it came to symbols of power and status. Gradually, he depended less on God and more on the props around him: the world's largest harem, a house twice the size of the temple, an army well-stocked with chariots, a strong economy.

Success may have eliminated any crisis of disappointment with God, but it also seemed to eliminate Solomon's desire for God at all. The more he enjoyed the world's good gifts, the less he thought about the Giver.

PHILIP YANCEY

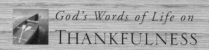

The trumpeters and singers joined in unison,
as with one voice, to give praise and thanks to the
LORD. Accompanied by trumpets, cymbals and
other instruments, they raised their voices in
praise to the LORD and sang: "He is good; his
love endures forever."

2 CHRONICLES 5:13

Praise the LORD.
Give thanks to the LORD, for he is good;
his love endures forever.

PSALM 106:1

Give thanks to the LORD, for he is good;
his love endures forever.
Let Israel say:
"His love endures forever."
Let the house of Aaron say:
"His love endures forever."
Let those who fear the LORD say:
"His love endures forever."

PSALM 118:1–4

Give thanks to the LORD, for he is good.
His love endures forever.
Give thanks to the God of gods.
His love endures forever.
Give thanks to the Lord of lords:
His love endures forever.

PSALM 136:1–3

Give thanks to the LORD, for he is good;
his love endures forever.

1 CHRONICLES 16:34

Let the peace of Christ rule in your hearts, since as members of one body you were called to peace. And be thankful. Let the word of Christ dwell in you richly as you teach and admonish one another with all wisdom, and as you sing psalms, hymns and spiritual songs with gratitude in your hearts to God. And whatever you do, whether in word or deed, do it all in the name of the Lord Jesus, giving thanks to God the Father through him.

COLOSSIANS 3:15–17

Devote yourselves to prayer, being watchful and thankful.

COLOSSIANS 4:2

Job said:

"Naked I came from my
mother's womb,
and naked I will depart.
The LORD gave and the LORD
has taken away;
may the name of the LORD
be praised."

In all this, Job did not sin by charging God with wrongdoing.

JOB 1:21–22

I will extol the LORD at all times;
his praise will always be on
my lips.

PSALM 34:1

Do not be anxious about anything, but in everything, by prayer and petition, with thanksgiving, present your requests to God.

PHILIPPIANS 4:6

Give thanks in all circumstances, for this is God's will for you in Christ Jesus.

1 THESSALONIANS 5:18

Thanks be to God! He gives us the victory through our Lord Jesus Christ.

1 CORINTHIANS 15:57

Thanks be to God for his indescribable gift!

2 CORINTHIANS 9:15

Give thanks to the LORD, call on his name;
make known among the nations
what he has done.

1 CHRONICLES 16:8

Praise the LORD.
I will extol the LORD with all my heart
in the council of the upright
and in the assembly.
Great are the works of the LORD;
they are pondered by all
who delight in them.

PSALM 111:1–2

Always giving thanks to God the Father for everything, in the name of our Lord Jesus Christ.

EPHESIANS 5:20

Rooted and built up in him, strengthened in the faith as you were taught, and overflowing with thankfulness.

COLOSSIANS 2:7

Sing to the LORD with thanksgiving;
*   make music to our God on the harp.*

PSALM 147:7

Enter his gates with thanksgiving
*   and his courts with praise;*
*   give thanks to him and*
*   praise his name.*

PSALM 100:4

I will sacrifice a thank offering to you
*   and call on the name of the LORD.*

PSALM 116:17

Since we are receiving a kingdom that cannot be shaken, let us be thankful, and so worship God acceptably with reverence and awe.

HEBREWS 12:28

Everything God created is good, and nothing is to be rejected if it is received with thanksgiving.

1 TIMOTHY 4:4

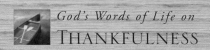
Through Jesus, therefore, let us continually offer to God a sacrifice of praise—the fruit of lips that confess his name.

HEBREWS 13:15

The LORD your God will bless you in all your harvest and in all the work of your hands, and your joy will be complete.

DEUTERONOMY 16:15

The sounds of joy and gladness, the voices of bride and bridegroom, and the voices of those who bring thank offerings to the house of the LORD, saying,

"Give thanks to the LORD Almighty,
for the LORD is good;
his love endures forever."

JEREMIAH 33:11

The magic of a thankful spirit is that it has the power to replace …

anger with love,

resentment with happiness,

fear with faith,

worry with peace,

the desire to dominate

with the wish to play on a team,

self-preoccupation

with concern for the needs of others,

guilt with an open door to forgiveness,

sexual impurity

with honor and respect,

jealousy with joy at another's success,

lack of creativity

with inspired productivity,

inferiorities with dignity,

a lack of love

with an abundance of self-sharing.

DONALD E. DEMARAY

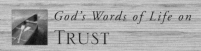
Those who know your name
will trust in you,
for you, LORD, have never
forsaken those who seek you.

PSALM 9:10

Abraham did not waver through unbelief regarding
the promise of God, but was strengthened in his
faith and gave glory to God, being fully persuaded
that God had power to do what he had promised.

ROMANS 4:20–21

Taste and see that the LORD is good;
blessed is the man who takes refuge in him.

PSALM 34:8

O LORD Almighty,
blessed is the man who trusts in you.

PSALM 84:12

Those who trust in the LORD
are like Mount Zion,
which cannot be shaken but
endures forever.

PSALM 125:1

Blessed is he whose help is the God of Jacob,
whose hope is in the LORD his God.

PSALM 146:5

Whoever gives heed to instruction prospers,
and blessed is he who trusts in the LORD.

PROVERBS 16:20

Blessed is the man who trusts in the LORD,
whose confidence is in him.
He will be like a tree planted by the water
that sends out its roots by the the stream.
It does not fear when heat comes;
its leaves are always green.
It has no worries in a year of drought
and never fails to bear fruit.

JEREMIAH 17:7–8

You will keep in perfect peace
him whose mind is steadfast,
because he trusts in you.
Trust in the LORD forever,
for the LORD, the LORD, is the Rock eternal.

ISAIAH 26:3–4

The LORD longs to be gracious to you;
he rises to show you compassion.
For the LORD is a God of justice.
Blessed are all who wait for him!

ISAIAH 30:18

Hezekiah trusted in the LORD, the God of Israel.
There was no one like him among all the kings of
Judah, either before him or after him.

2 KINGS 18:5

The LORD's unfailing love
surrounds the man who
trusts in him.

PSALM 32:10

Trust in the LORD and do good;
    dwell in the land and enjoy safe pasture.
Delight yourself in the LORD
    and he will give you the desires of your heart.
Commit your way to the LORD;
    trust in him and he will do this:
He will make your righteousness
        shine like the dawn,
    the justice of your cause like the noonday sun.

PSALM 37:3–6

Blessed is the man
    who makes the LORD his trust,
who does not look to the proud,
    to those who turn aside to false gods.

PSALM 40:4

Nebuchadnezzar said, "Praise be to the God of Shadrach, Meshach and Abednego, who has sent his angel and rescued his servants! They trusted in him and defied the king's command and were willing to give up their lives rather than serve or worship any god except their own God."

DANIEL 3:28

A greedy man stirs up dissension,
    but he who trusts in the
        LORD will prosper.

PROVERBS 28:25

Anyone who trusts in [God] will never be put to shame.

ROMANS 10:11

Be strong and take heart,
  all you who hope in the LORD.

PSALM 31:24

Fear of man will prove to be a snare,
  but whoever trusts in the
    LORD is kept safe.

PROVERBS 29:25

When you pass through the waters,
  I will be with you;
and when you pass through the rivers,
  they will not sweep over you.
When you walk through the fire,
  you will not be burned;
  the flames will not set you ablaze.

ISAIAH 43:2

The LORD is good,
  a refuge in times of trouble.
He cares for those who trust in him.

NAHUM 1:7

The LORD bless you and keep you;
the LORD make his face shine upon you
  and be gracious to you;
the LORD turn his face toward you
  and give you peace.

NUMBERS 6:24–26

To you, O LORD, I lift up my soul;
in you I trust, O my God.
Do not let me be put to shame,
nor let my enemies triumph over me.
No one whose hope is in you
will ever be put to shame.

PSALM 25:1-3

Offer right sacrifices
and trust in the LORD.
Many are asking, "Who can
show us any good?"
Let the light of your face
shine upon us, O LORD.
You have filled my heart with
greater joy
than when their grain and
new wine abound.
I will lie down and sleep in peace,
for you alone, O LORD,
make me dwell in safety.

PSALM 4:5-8

Trust in the LORD with all your heart
and lean not on your own understanding;
in all your ways acknowledge him,
and he will make your paths straight.

PROVERBS 3:5-6

We used to play a game at summer camp in which we would blindfold one of the kids and have him or her run through a wooded area, relying on a friend for verbal directions to help navigate. "Turn to the left; there's a tree coming!" "There's a log in front of you—jump!" Some kids would not trust the verbal directions whatsoever. They would shuffle their feet and walk very slowly, even though their friends were shouting that the way was clear. Other kids would trot along, and a few would go like gangbusters.

As Christians, we sometimes feel like those blindfolded children. We are not alone in the woods, though—God will direct our paths. But quite often his leadings sound illogical, irrational, countercultural. Sometimes he is so challenging that I say, "No, I think I'll just crawl back into my shell and play it safe." Then a voice inside me says, "Where's your courage, Hybels? Get up and walk. You can trust God."

It takes enormous courage to follow God's leadings in the Christian life. Some of his callings demand the best that you can summon. Some of his tests stretch you to the limit. Truly, spiritual courage or trust is on the endangered character-quality list.

BILL HYBELS

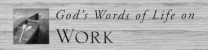
Six days do your work, but on the seventh day
do not work, so that your ox and your donkey
may rest and the slave born in your household,
and the alien as well, may be refreshed.

EXODUS 23:12

From the fruit of his lips a man is
filled with good things
as surely as the work of his
hands rewards him.

PROVERBS 12:14

May the favor of the Lord our
God rest upon us;
establish the work of our
hands for us—
yes, establish the work of
our hands.

PSALM 90:17

Lazy hands make a man poor,
but diligent hands bring wealth.

PROVERBS 10:4

Whatever your hand finds to do, do it with all
your might, for in the grave, where you are going,
there is neither working nor planning nor
knowledge nor wisdom.

ECCLESIASTES 9:10

The sluggard craves and gets nothing,
but the desires of the diligent are fully satisfied.

PROVERBS 13:4

All hard work brings a profit,
    but mere talk leads only to poverty.
PROVERBS 14:23

The laborer's appetite works for him;
    his hunger drives him on.
PROVERBS 16:26

The plans of the diligent lead to profit
    as surely as haste leads to poverty.
PROVERBS 21:5

Do you see a man skilled in his work?
    He will serve before kings;
    he will not serve before obscure men.
PROVERBS 22:29

My heart took delight in all my work,
    and this was the reward for all my labor.
ECCLESIASTES 2:10

Sow your seed in the morning,
    and at evening let not your hands be idle,
for you do not know which will succeed,
    whether this or that,
    or whether both will do equally well.
ECCLESIASTES 11:6

Make it your ambition to lead a quiet life, to mind your own business and to work with your hands, just as we told you, so that your daily life may win the respect of outsiders and so that you will not be dependent on anybody.
1 THESSALONIANS 4:11–12

Even when we were with you, we gave you this
rule: "If a man will not work, he shall not eat."
2 THESSALONIANS 3:10

By the sweat of your brow
you will eat your food
until you return to the ground,
since from it you were taken;
for dust you are
and to dust you will return.
GENESIS 3:19

Do not take advantage of a hired man who is poor
and needy, whether he is a brother Israelite or an
alien living in one of your towns. Pay him his
wages each day before sunset, because he is poor
and is counting on it. Otherwise he may cry to the
LORD against you, and you will be guilty of sin.
DEUTERONOMY 24:14–15

Jesus said, "The man who had received the five
talents brought the other five. 'Master,' he said,
'you entrusted me with five talents. See, I have
gained five more.' His master replied, 'Well done,
good and faithful servant! You have been faithful
with a few things; I will put you in charge of many
things. Come and share your master's happiness!'"
MATTHEW 25:20–21

When a man works, his wages are not credited to
him as a gift, but as an obligation.
ROMANS 4:4

Many workers today are sacrificing themselves on the altar of work. They tolerate immensely harmful symptoms such as anger, chemical dependencies and loneliness in a blind pursuit of self-fulfillment through career success. This may be pathological—but it is also idolatrous! Such a person worships his career as though it were a god.

But like all idols, work is impotent in the face of true human need. I have sat with grown men, exceptionally powerful men in business, and watched them weep as they told me their tragic stories, some with personal lives shattered, others with families in shambles, perhaps their character debased or their circumstances out of control. None of their professional accomplishments, none of the machinery of their companies, none of their wealth is of the slightest help. They are in deep trouble and their god is impotent.

I grieve with such men. I also respect the fact that the same thing could happen to me as to anyone. It happens when we take God's gift of work and begin to worship and serve it rather than Christ.

DOUG SHERMAN AND WILLIAM HENDRICKS

Share Your Thoughts

With the Author: Your comments will be forwarded to the author when you send them to *zauthor@zondervan.com*.

With Zondervan: Submit your review of this book by writing to *zreview@zondervan.com*.

Free Online Resources at
www.zondervan.com/hello

 Zondervan AuthorTracker: Be notified whenever your favorite authors publish new books, go on tour, or post an update about what's happening in their lives.

 Daily Bible Verses and Devotions: Enrich your life with daily Bible verses or devotions that help you start every morning focused on God.

 Free Email Publications: Sign up for newsletters on fiction, Christian living, church ministry, parenting, and more.

 Zondervan Bible Search: Find and compare Bible passages in a variety of translations at www.zondervanbiblesearch.com.

 Other Benefits: Register yourself to receive online benefits like coupons and special offers, or to participate in research.